AN ILLUSTRATED BIOGRAPHY OF C. G. JUNG

AN ILLUSTRATED BIOGRAPHY OF

C. G. JUNG

Gerhard Wehr

Translated by Michael H. Kohn

SHAMBHALA
Boston & Shaftesbury
1989

Shambhala Publications, Inc.
Horticultural Hall
300 Massachusetts Avenue
Boston, Massachusetts 02115

Shambhala Publications Inc.
The Old School House
The Courtyard, Bell Street
Shaftesbury, Dorset SP7 8BP

9 8 7 6 5 4 3 2 1

First Edition

Graphic Art:
Franz Gisler

Composition by
F. X. Stückle,
D-7637 Ettenheim

Photolithography by
Schwitter AG, Allschwil,
Switzerland

Printed by
Arts Graphiques
Héliographia SA,
Lausanne, Switzerland

Printed in Switzerland

Distributed in the United States by Random House and in Canada by Random House of Canada Ltd.
Distributed in the United Kingdom by Element Books Ltd.

Library of Congress
Cataloging-in-Publication
Data
Wehr, Gerhard.
An illustrated biography of C. G. Jung / Gerhard Wehr
p. cm.
ISBN 0-87773-510-7
1. Jung, C. G. (Carl Gustav), 1875 – 1961. 2. Psychoanalysts – Austria – Biography. I. Title.
BF109.J8W44 1989
150. 19'54 – dc 20 89-42630
[B] CIP

THE EARLY YEARS

FIRST EXPERIENCE IN DEPTH PSYCHOLOGY

LAYING THE FOUNDATIONS OF ANALYTICAL PSYCHOLOGY

LATER WORK AND FURTHER PERSPECTIVES

Jung’s ex libris with the motto that appears over the door of his Küsnacht residence and on his gravestone: Vocatus atque non vocatus deus aderit *(Called or not called, the god will be there).*

Page 2: C. G. Jung in a portrait of 1937.

Opposite: Jung at his desk, at which he composed a good many of his voluminous works (1952).

This painting by C. G. Jung was done in 1904, during a period when he frequently had recourse to brush and palette to preserve his impressions without associating a particular psychological intention with them.

"The name Jung seldom leaves people cold. When one mentions this man, one almost always encounters emotionally charged rejection or enthusiasm, rarely an objective judgment. Looking more closely, one realizes that this reaction is really aimed at the unconscious – that god or demon whose existence so many people today do not wish to admit. This is why they raise such petty objections to depth psychology, not realizing that they are acting out of fear. Thus Jung's work lies like a stumbling block in the midst of contemporary works of the mind – in a certain way, far too essential and fundamental to be modern."[1]

This remark by Marie-Louise von Franz, for many years a close collaborator of Carl Gustav Jung, is thoughtprovoking. We must ask ourselves, is this the proper assessment of the man who, along with Sigmund Freud, made depth psychology into a fundamental science that opened many new perspectives?

The uncontested credit for laying the scientific groundwork of modern psychiatry indubitably goes to Sigmund Freud. It was Freud, as he himself saw it, who in the wake of Copernicus and Darwin, visited upon modern man his third great insult or fall from glory by laying bare the structure of human motivation and destroying the one-sided idealistic view of man as a being controlled by his own consciousness.

But in comparison with Freud's work, Jung's own independent contribution, which opened up entirely new dimensions of reality, has never received the recognition that might be expected. As recently as 1975, on the occasion of the centennial of Jung's birth, it was pointed out that Jung's work is "today at best only partially known," hardly taught in academic institutions and little heeded in research.

Nevertheless interest in the approach, methods, and results of analytical psychology is on the rise. This is especially the case for disciplines and domains of knowledge outside of psychology. And what

about psychotherapy? In an interview for the Swiss weekly Die Weltwoche, Jung characterized himself and his work as follows:

"I am a doctor involved with the illness of the people of his time, mindful of remedies that correspond to the reality of the ailment. Psychopathological research has brought me to awaken historical symbols and figures out of the dust of their tombs. I have seen that it is not enough to make the symptoms of my patients go away. ... We are not so much in need of ideals as of a little wisdom and introspection, careful religious consideration of experiences from the unconscious. I use the term "religious" advisedly, because it seems to me that these experiences that help to make life healthier or more beautiful, or to shape it more completely or more meaningfully for oneself or one's loved ones are of sufficient magnitude so that one can say about them: it was the grace of God."[2]

This personal reflection on the part of the depth psychologist shows how Jung as a doctor and as a scientific-minded psychologist was bound by the way in which he conceived his duty as a healer continually to go beyond the limitations of his discipline.

The accomplishment of his work as a whole is not so much related to any special field but rather has to do with that central knowledge that touches upon all aspects of life and understanding – the knowledge of the Self and the world.

In sum, analytical psychology is first and foremost a contribution toward a universal vision of reality that encompasses the individual and the world, mind and matter. It is on the universal applicability of Jung's work that its relevance for us rests. If the result of this is that nowadays not only professionally trained psychotherapists but lay persons as well are making use of Jungian terminology, the need is all the greater to gain a more precise knowledge of his life, his work, and his influence.

THE EARLY YEARS

EARLY LIFE: "THE PSYCHE IS NOT OF THE PRESENT!"

Carl Gustav Jung, the son of a Swiss Reformed Evangelical minister, Johann Paul Achilles Jung, and his wife, Emilie, née Preiswerk, was born 26 July, 1875, in Kesswil, a small rural township near Romanshorn in the Thurgau on Lake Constance. Because both his father and mother possessed Basel citizenship from birth, he is also considered a citizen of this tradition-rich city, in which men of the intellectual stature of Paracelsus and Friedrich Nietzsche lived for short periods. Jung, in his later career as a psychotherapist, a doctor of the soul, was to discover his relationship with both of these men.

His parents came from hardly less tradition-rich families. His mother came from the reputable Preiswerk family, a family of Protestant ministers. His father, who had degrees in philology and theology, was the son of the Basel physician and professor Carl Gustav Jung the elder, born in Mainz. Because Jung always felt an inner relationship to this grandfather of the same name, though he never knew him personally, it is worth saying a word or two about him.

Carl Gustav Jung the elder was involved with a group of student fraternities that in 1817, on the occasion of the three hundredth anniversary of the Reformation, occupied the Wartburg castle. Together, students and professors demonstrated for a unified Germany. The young follower of this earlier student protest movement was arrested and, without due process of law, imprisoned for thirteen months. Later, no less a personage than Alexander von Humboldt recommended the prospective physician for entrance into the University of Basel. Grandfather Jung was highly regarded as a physician and a university professor, as a humanist and a philanthropist.

Samuel Preiswerk, Jung's maternal grandfather, also enjoyed high esteem. He

The house in Kesswil in Thurgau Canton where Jung was born (photograph taken about 1900).

Opposite: Carl Gustav with his parents and his sister Gertrud (about 1893).

Pages 10 and 11: Aerial view of Basel (about 1865).

was pastor of the Leonhard parish of Basel and at the same time held the office of Antistes, or head vicar of the reformed ministry there.

But what is the significance of ancestry and kinship? Jung provides food for reflection for people who are interested in genealogy:

"The psyche is not of the present! Its age is to be counted in the millions of years. The individual consciousness is only the flower and fruit of a season that grows out of the perennial rhizome under the earth, and it finds itself better attuned to the truth when it takes the existence of the rhizome into account, for the root system is the mother of all."[3]

The two grandfathers: left, the physician and university professor Carl Gustav Jung (1794–1864): right, the chief rector from Basel, Samuel Preiswerk (1799–1871).

To this notion of a transpersonal, collective, basic constituent of human existence, Jung added a further aspect. This was at first an unformed presentiment, which became the knowledge, growing ever clearer, of our "double origin." Jung referred to "No. 1" – the C. G. Jung that the world around him saw, and "No. 2" – the one who existed in the depths of his being, a being that pointed beyond his daily existence. With this presentiment and this knowledge, depth psychology came into its own.

In his autobiography, *Memories, Dreams, Reflections,* which he described – like his life as a whole – as "the story of a self-realization of the unconscious," he clearly explains how inadequate is a biography that remains in the foreground and considers only the external facts. Something primordial is seeking to attain incarnation in every individual. Hence Jung's observation, which in his notes he applies at least to himself:

"What we are to our inward vision, and what to man appears to be *sub specie aeternitatis,* can only be expressed by way of myth. Myth is more individual and expresses life more precisely than does science. Science works with concepts of averages which are far too general to do justice to the subjective variety of an individual life."[4]

Myth manifested itself in the everyday life of the growing boy, and then, in the form of particular inner experiences, it accompanied the development of the adult psychotherapist, punctuating it with meaning all the way to the end. For little Carl Gustav, it began with life in the family of a rural parson in the little town of Laufen, hard by the Rhine Falls, near Schaffhausen. This is the point that his memories reach back to. There was the simple village parsonage, the garden, a nearby castle, the waterfall, and the sexton's farm. A wealth of elementary experiences awaited. The deepest impressions came from being close to nature, from contact with stones, plants, and animals, and from the fascination that water can bring. The boy always felt himself surrounded by the sphere of the enigmatic, the mysterious. Hence the words of the autobiographer: "My whole youth can be understood in terms of the concept of mystery." Only his youth? Anyone who knew Jung well – his highly developed sense of intuition through which he forged ahead as a psychotherapist and a researcher in the border regions of human knowledge – ascribed magical or mediumistic powers to him, not to mention an astonishing level of knowledge in many fields. Thus, as an old man writing his memoirs, he added these words: "Still today, I am lonely, because I know, and must speak of, things that others do not know and for the most part by no means wish to know."

His immediate surroundings – the parsonage, the church, the graveyard – became a realm of mystery for the boy about the time he first became consciously aware of what the sexton did and what took place in the graveyard. A deep hole would be dug. Men in black frock coats with measured steps would bring a box and set it in the ground. Women would cry and lament. There would be talk of a burial, and his own father, also in a long black clerical gown, was part of it! This had its problematic side, because the man in the box would never appear again. People would say, "Lord Jesus" had taken him to himself. "I began to distrust Lord Jesus. He lost the aspect of a big, comforting, benevolent bird and became associated with the gloomy black men in frock coats, top hats, and shiny black boots who busied themselves with the black box. These ruminations of mine led to my first conscious trauma."[5]

Dreams would also soon belong to his world of mystery. A dream from those early years, the scene of which was a meadow not far from his parents' house, made an indelible impression on Jung. Not until he was sixty-five years old did Jung recount this childhood dream and indicate its importance. Here again we are involved with a hole in the ground, a dark, rectangular hole, walled in stone. Jung tells us:

"I ran forward and curiously peered down into it. Then I saw a stone stairway leading down. Hesitantly and fearfully, I descended. At the bottom was a doorway with a round arch, closed off by a green curtain. It was a big, heavy curtain of worked stuff like brocade, and it looked very sumptuous. Curious to see what might be hidden behind, I pushed it aside. I saw before me in the dim light a rectangular chamber about thirty feet long. The ceiling was arched and of hewn stone. The floor was laid with flagstones, and in the center a red carpet ran from the entrance to a low platform. On this platform stood a wonderfully rich golden throne. I am not certain, but perhaps a red cushion lay on the seat. It was a magnificent throne, a real king's throne in a fairy tale. Something was standing on it which I thought at first was a tree trunk twelve to fifteen feet high and about one and a half to two feet thick. It was a huge thing, reaching almost to the ceiling. But it was of a curious composition: it was made of skin and naked flesh, and on the top there was something like a rounded head with no face and no hair. On the very top of the head was a single eye, gazing motionlessly upward."[6]

*Jung's parents Paul and Emilie Jung (*née *Preiswerk) as a young couple.*

Many years were to go by before the dreamer gained some insight into the meaning of the strange image. It was not until he was an experienced psychothera-

"A half-year after my birth, my parents moved from Kesswil on Lake Constance to the parsonage of Laufen Castle above the Falls of the Rhine." The castle and church in 1876.

pist, skilled in working with symbols, that he knew that the young boy had been confronted by the creative principle in the form of a ritual phallus. Jung's interpretation runs: "Through this childhood dream, I was being introduced to the mystery of the earth. . . . It was like a kind of initiation into the realm of darkness." Here he is referring to that darkness that is an integral part of reality as a whole and therefore must not be denied.

A key role in the life of Jung must doubtless be ascribed to this "great dream." It is as though the essential structure of his personality had relaxed, making him more receptive toward the images, formations, and events of an "inescapable world of shadows" that poses problems of knowledge that must be solved by the person who is confronted by them. Ever new data of this kind presented themselves to Jung over the years. The boundary between "this side" and "the beyond," between the conscious and the unconscious, became a permeable one. An eternal world lay beneath the transitory one. It is no wonder that later on Jung considered recollection of external facts not very important. In any case, they were growing faint for him.

"But my encounters with the 'other' reality, my bouts with the unconscious, are indelibly engraved upon my memory. In that realm there has always been wealth in abundance, and everything else has lost importance by comparison. . . . My dreams and visions. These form the fiery magma out of which the stone that had to be worked was crystallized."[7]

Reading this, Jung's task in life seems to have been programmed in advance from the beginning. Freud had already set out in pursuit of a similar leitmotiv: if I cannot subdue the gods above, then I will stir up the gods of the depths.

But how different Jung's prospects appeared! He was the son of a father who, as a minister, served a god in whom he himself was unable to believe:

"Theology had alienated my father and me from one another. . . . I had a dim premonition that he was inescapably succumbing to his fate. He was lonely and had no friend to talk with. At least I knew no one among our acquaintances whom I would have trusted to say the saving word. Once I heard him praying. He struggled desperately to keep his faith. I was shaken and outraged at once, because I saw how hopelessly he was entrapped by the Church and its theological thinking."[8]

"I no longer remember our move to Klein-Hüningen near Basel in 1879 . . ." The parsonage in Klein-Hüningen, from which Jung as a student traveled to the Gymnasium in Basel.

Jung's father received a new position as a parson in Klein-Hüningen near Basel. This was to be the scene of the events of the next years. Carl Gustav attended the Gymnasium in Basel. The son of the village parson, who lived on a portion of modest church revenues, now for the first time inhaled the atmosphere of the "world" in this city of, at that time, only about fifty thousand inhabitants. The year was 1886. At the same time he became aware of social differences as he saw numbers of his schoolmates riding up "in costly carriages with wonderful horses." He himself had to cover the several kilometers to school on foot. His simple uniform could not at all compare to their chic school wardrobes. Worn-out shoes with holes in the soles and darned socks were his lot. But this was not the source of Carl Gustav's problems. Rather it was the marital discord that his parents were unable to hide from him that was burdening him. As for the school situation itself, the novice scholar experienced some difficulties with abstract thinking of the type that is required, for example, in mathematics. "The teacher pretended that algebra was a perfectly natural affair, to be taken for granted, whereas I didn't even know what numbers really were. They were not flowers, not animals, not fossils; they were nothing that could be imagined, mere quantities that resulted from counting. . . . To my horror I found that no one understood my difficulty."[9]

The parson's son found the divinity lessons "extremely boring." Even the confirmation lessons he received from his father did not fare better in the pupil's judgment. Anything to do with the church or dogma that was presented to him in these years only brought on malaise, precisely because another kind of spirituality, attuned to the mysteries of the earth, was filling the growing boy. But for this he found no understanding in the world around him, neither from his father nor from his uncles, who were also parsons. His mother, who had introduced him to prayer in his early childhood, was closest to having some instinctive understanding of the world in which her son was living. Jung recalls the following in *Memories, Dreams, Reflections:*

Jung as a medical student at the University of Basel during the winter semester of 1896 – 97.
"I was struck by the illuminating thought that I could study medicine. Curiously, this had never occurred to me before, despite the fact that my paternal grandfather, of whom I had heard so much, was also a doctor. It was just on this account that I had certain resistances toward this profession."

"At that time, too, there arose in me profound doubts about everything my father said. When I heard him preaching about grace, I always thought of my own experience. What he said sounded stale and hollow, like a tale told by someone who knows it only by hearsay and cannot quite believe it himself. ... I wanted to help him but I did not know how ... He did not know the immediate living God who stands omnipotent and free above His Bible and His Church, who calls upon man to partake of His freedom, and can force him to renounce his own views and convictions in order to fulfill without reserve the command of God ... In His trial of human courage God refuses to abide by traditions, no matter how sacred. In his omnipotence he will see to it that nothing really evil comes from such tests of courage. If one fulfills the will of God one can be sure of going the right way."[10]

No wonder that we hear from Jung about occasional depressions that overshadowed his time of puberty. This did not improve until he was sixteen or seventeen. At that point school became more interesting. Particularly the great figures of intellectual history drew his interest. "I began systematically pursuing questions I had consciously framed. ... Above all I was attracted to the thought of Pythagoras, Heraclitus, Empedocles, and Plato, despite the long-windedness of Socratic argumentations." By contrast, the philosophical thought of Thomas Aquinas and the scholastic approach left him cold. Much more interesting was Schopenhauer, though this did not mean at all that the young reader agreed with his views. The fascination that the underground, dark, mysterious aspect of life can exercise on a person need not fill him with gloom.

Preparation for a Career

All these factors affecting his later life have been vividly presented by Jung in his autobiographical writings. Under their influence, and considering the Gymnasium student's very particular interests, he now had to decide what direction his studies would take after graduation. Carl had begun to collect all manner of Jurassic fossils and minerals. Zoology and biology were among his favorite subjects at school. On the other side, he was fascinated by archaeology, and not less by religious and intellectual history. In the natural sciences, it was concrete phenomena and the process leading up to them through earlier stages of development that gave him satisfaction; on the religious side, it was certain intellectual problems.

When Jung matriculated at the University of Basel on 18 April 1895, he chose the faculty of medicine. This was the same faculty in which his grandfather Carl Gustav had been active, and also, for a short time in the sixteenth century, Paracelsus. It was when he encountered the 1890 edition of Richard von Krafft-Ebing's textbook of psychiatry that it became clear to the prospective physician that the field of psychiatry and psychiatric research would be the one that would best enable him to pursue his inclinations toward both science and the humanities. Already the first lines of the textbook had an indelible effect on the young reader. Jung tells us:

"My heart suddenly began to pound. I had to stand up and draw a deep breath. My excitement was intense, for it had become clear to me, in a flash of illumination, that for me the only possible goal was psychiatry. Here alone the two currents of my interest could flow together and in a united stream dig their own bed. Here was the empirical field common to biological and spiritual facts, which I had everywhere sought and nowhere found. Here at last was the place where the collision of nature and spirit became a reality."[11]

Jung – who is depicted as a highly gregarious student and, as a member of the Swiss student society Zofingia, an enthusiastic dancer – lived during this time in penury. With the early death in 1896 of his father, the parsonage house had to be given up. With his mother and his sister Johanna Gertrud (1884 – 1935), nine years his junior, he found a modest dwelling in the neighborhood of Bottminger Mill, near Basel. The Jungs had no savings. Also there was no financial provision for the surviving members of the family such as might have been expected from the church. To finance at least a part of Jung's studies, an uncle came forward with a loan to his nephew in the amount of three thousand francs, a considerable sum for the turn of the century. This had to be paid off a little at a time. "I would not have missed this time of poverty," Jung admits in retrospect. "One learns to value simple things. I still remember the time when I was given a box of cigars as a present. It seemed to me princely. They lasted a whole year, for I allowed myself one

LEHRBUCH

DER

PSYCHIATRIE

AUF KLINISCHER GRUNDLAGE

FÜR

PRAKTISCHE ÄRZTE UND STUDIRENDE

VON

DR. R. v. KRAFFT-EBING,

K. K. O. Ö. PROFESSOR DER PSYCHIATRIE UND DER NERVENKRANKHEITEN AN DER UNIVERSITÄT WIEN.

Vierte theilweise umgearbeitete Auflage.

STUTTGART.
VERLAG VON FERDINAND ENKE.
1890.

Dr. Richard von Krafft-Ebing (1840 – 1902) and his textbook of psychiatry, which was a key factor in Jung's choice of a specialty.
"Here alone the two currents of my interest could flow together and in a united stream dig their own bed. Here was the empirical field common to biological and spiritual facts, which I had everywhere sought and nowhere found."

Above: From left to right, Aunt Auguste ("Gusteli"), Emilie Jung, and Sophie Fröhlich.

Below: Bottminger Mill near Basel, where widow Jung lived with her two children during Carl's student days.

only on Sundays."[12] Already in the early semesters, the student began to take on all kinds of odd jobs in order to provide essential support.

An area of exploration and research that was to be important to Jung began already in these early years to open up for him. This was the field of parapsychology, dealing with so-called occult phenomena. Especially on his mother's side, a certain affinity with this kind of phenomena can be observed. We may also mention Jung's early interest in the literature on this subject, for example, the work of the eighteenth-century Norwegian "seer of spirits" Emanuel Swedenborg; and from the nineteenth century, Justinus Kerner's *Die Seherin von Prevorst* (The Seeress of Prevorst). "The observations of the spiritualists, weird and questionable as they seemed to me, were the first accounts I had seen of objective psychic pheno-

The Preiswerk children. On the right Helly, who functioned as a medium.

Sitzung den 18. August 1897

Abends 8½ h bei K. G. Jung, Bottminger Mühle.

Controllierende Teilnehmer: R. Gonser stud. med.
A. Müller stud. med.
K. G. Jung stud. med.
E. Preiswerk stud. phil.
C. R. Stachelin cand. med.

A. Versuche mit dem Glas

1. Frage: Was hältst du von der Sünde?

Antwort: „Sie ist das Verderben der Menschen schon Anfangs gewesen."

2. Frage: Ist die Stelle V Mose 18, 11 gegen den Spiritismus gerichtet?

Antwort: „Nein"

3. Frage: Hat diese Stelle Bedeutung für uns?

Antwort: „Sie geht euch gar nichts an."

4. Frage: Ist es Zeit um Experimente mit dem Tisch anfangen zu können?

Antwort: „Ja"

B. Versuche mit dem Tisch

Bewegungen mit und ohne Berührungen, Drehungen, In die Höhe heben (ca 50 cm).

Minutes of the spiritualist séance of August 18, 1897, in which Jung participated with four students. The theological questions are directed to deceased grandfather Preiswerk.

mena. ... For myself I found such possibilities extremely interesting and attractive. They added another dimension to my life; the world gained depth and background."[13]

One of Jung's early convictions, which he held in principle for the rest of his life, was the insight that our picture of the world corresponds to reality only to the extent that it has a place in it for the improbable. And indeed it was not long before a curious phenomenon took place.

It was during the summer break. In the house near the Bottminger Mill, Emilie Jung was sitting in her armchair knitting. Nearby, her son Carl sat pondering over his books. Suddenly from the dining room came a bang "like a pistol shot." They were quite astonished to find that the tabletop "had split through all the way past the middle, and by no means at a glued joint, but through the solid wood."

Hardly two weeks later, another such incident took place. As Jung entered the house, he found the family in a state of great excitement. Another such "shot" had occurred. This time the bread knife had been found in the drawer, for the most part in pieces. "The handle lay in one corner of the rectangular basket, and in each of the other corners lay a piece of the blade. The knife had been used shortly before, at four-o'clock tea and afterward put away. Since then no one had gone to the sideboard." Without considering that such phenomena may sometimes occur in the vicinity of a young person in puberty – his sister Gertrud was about 14 years

Spiritualist séance led by Arthur Houghton (about 1870).

old – Jung let his suspicion fall upon another young girl. This was "Helly" (Helene Preiswerk, 1881–1911), a maternal cousin,[14] who served as a medium in the spiritualistic seances that were held in the family circle on Saturday evenings. Jung was against these sessions. His mother and Helly's, however, after initial hesitation, came to favor them, because during them Parson Samuel Preiswerk, highly respected by all, appeared to speak as the "guide and guardian of the medium." The decidedly rationalistic grandfather Carl Gustav, by contrast, had earlier on been in the habit of denouncing spiritualistic activities as sheer nonsense. His grandson not only gave these goings-on his full attention, but went on to make the events at Bottminger Mill the object of a scientific investigation. The results can be found in Jung's doctoral thesis, presented to the medical faculty of the University of Zurich under the title, "On the Psychology and Pathology of So-called Occult Phenomena." Of course the author deliberately avoided mentioning the name of Helene Preiswerk. The dissertation speaks of her only as "Miss S. W." For the doctoral candidate, this was a "case of somnambulism in a disturbed person." In order not to compromise the scientific character of his thesis, the author avoided indicating the manner in which he himself had become involved in the matter.

Left: Séance at the house of Meister Casparin (about 1880).

When this dissertation appeared in print in Leipzig in 1902, the title page bore the phrase "Approved at the request of Prof. E. Bleuler." And the author already gave his title as "first assistant physician in the Burghölzli Clinic." This refers to the site of Jung's first medical activity in Zurich (in 1900 he had received his license to practice medicine throughout Switzerland). This meant leaving Basel.

3"I was glad to be in Zurich, for in the course of the years Basel had become too stuffy for me. For the Baslers no town exists but their own: only Basel is 'civilized', and north of the river Birs the land of the barbarians begins. ... In Basel I was stamped for all time as the son of the Reverend Paul Jung and the grandson of Professor Carl Gustav Jung. I was an intellectual and belonged to a definite social set. I felt resistances against this, for I could not and would not let myself be classified."[15]

But with this move, he did establish a definite reference point for himself, at least as far as his choice of residence is concerned – Lake Zurich. For there he was to live from then on, whether in Zurich itself or in neighboring Küsnacht. Even his private refuge, the ominous tower of Bollingen, stands on the shores of his beloved lake. Jung never made any secret of the importance for him, since earliest childhood, of living in contact with the elements, particularly water.

Below: Basel showing the bank of the Rhine along the Augustinergasse (1880 – 1890).

Schweizerische Eidgenossenschaft

Diplom

Nachdem Herr Karl Jung aus Basel die reglementarische Prüfung zur Ausübung der ärztlichen Praxis vor der Prüfungs-Kommission zu Basel bestanden hat, wird ihm hierdurch die Berechtigung erteilt, seinen Beruf als

Arzt

in allen Kantonen der Schweiz in Gemäßheit des Art. 1 des Bundesgesetzes vom 19. Christmonat 1877 betreffend die Freizügigkeit des Medizinalpersonals in der schweizerischen Eidgenossenschaft auszuüben.

Bern, den 27. November 1900.

Der Vorsteher des eidgen. Departement des Innern:

Der Präsident des leitenden Ausschusses:

Der Präsident der Prüfungskommission:

Zur

Psychologie und Pathologie

sogenannter occulter Phänomene.

Inaugural-Dissertation

zur

Erlangung der Doktorwürde
einer Hohen medicinischen Facultät
der Universität Zürich

vorgelegt

von

C. G. Jung

I. Assistenzarzt an der Heilanstalt Burghölzli.

Genehmigt auf Antrag

des Herrn Professor Dr. E. Bleuler.

Leipzig
Druck von Oswald Mutze.
1902.

Above: Jung's medical degree (1900) and the title page from his medical school dissertation, published in 1902.

Left: Dr. Eugen Bleuler (1857 – 1939), the head of the Burghölzli Clinic.

Below right: Jung as assistant physician at Dr. Bleuler's clinic.

The Young Psychiatrist

The move to Zurich was a decisive turning point in Jung's professional life. Since its founding in 1860 Burghölzli, a psychiatric clinic connected with the University of Zurich, had earned a good reputation in medical circles. Under the leadership of Jung's doctoral sponsor, Prof. Eugen Bleuler (1857 – 1939), who was professor of psychiatry at the University of Zurich from 1898 to 1927, the exemplary quality of the clinic, which it reached under his predecessor Auguste Henri Forel (1848 – 1931), was heightened still further. Along with the physician Emil Kraepelin in Munich, Bleuler could be considered the leading light of psychiatry at the time. He was reputed to be full of humanity and kindness as a doctor with his patients and as a mentor to young doctors, an inspiring figure who inspired them to give their all. At the beginning of the twentieth century, a period of fundamentally new perspectives in the humanities, Bleuler attempted to understand the mentally disturbed patients in all aspects of their behavior. For him, understanding meant to penetrate to the essential core of the person, and this meant to respect as a person a patient whose plight was precisely that of being divested of human dignity.

He was altogether an exemplary master for Jung, who was at the very beginning of his medical and scientific career. As a beginner, he was willing to submit to the stern discipline that Bleuler demanded from all his colleagues and assistants. This included living in the clinic in order to be as close to the patients as possible. Every doctor at Burghölzli had to submit to a strict regimen of life and work. Some of them spoke of a "secular monastery," which left the individual hardly any freedom. Other colleagues of Jung's, later

partisans of the Zurich analyst Alphonse Maeder, characterized the situation at Burghölzli as follows:

"Burghölzli at that time was a kind of factory where you worked a lot and were paid a little. Everybody, from the professor down to the youngest assistant, was fully taken up with his work. Everybody was forced to abstain from alcoholic beverages. ... The patient was the focal point of interest. The student learned how he had to speak with him."[16]

Clearly, Jung submitted to all this without objection. He was very much the apprentice who could not penetrate fast enough and deep enough into the fundaments and abysses of the human psyche and of psychiatry itself. On top of the clinical regimen, there was also personal study. The assistant doctor, who soon gained the trust of his chief, acquainted himself with all the professional literature. For example, he read through the entirety of the fifty volumes of the *Allgemeinen Zeitschrift für Psychiatrie* (General Journal of psychiatry). His goal was clear:

"I wanted to know how the human mind reacted to the sight of its own destruction, for psychiatry seemed to me an articulate expression of that biological reaction which seizes upon the so-called healthy mind in the presence of mental illness. My professional colleagues seemed to me no less interesting than the patients. ... The years at Burghölzli were my years of apprenticeship. Dominating my interests and research was the burning question: "What actually takes place inside the mentally ill?" That was something which I did not understand then, nor had any of my colleagues concerned themselves with such problems. Psychiatry teachers were not interested in what the patient had to say, but rather in how to make a diagnosis or how to describe symptoms and to compile statistics. From the clinical point of view which then prevailed, the human personality of the patient, his individuality, did not matter at all. Rather, the doctor was confronted with Patient X, with a long list of cut-and-dried diagnoses and a detailing of symptoms. Patients, were labeled, rubber-stamped with a diagnosis."[17]

Jung followed in the footsteps of his master insofar as he also sought to find meaning and personal value in the horrid and frightening symptoms of psychosis and imbecility exhibited by the patients assigned to him. Little by little he reached the insight that what people thought they

Above: The Salpêtrière in Paris (about 1900): formerly a psychiatric center of international repute.

Below: The psychiatrist Pierre Janet (1859–1947), with whom Jung studied.

"I knew with absolute certainty she would be my wife." Emma Rauschenbach.

were discovering in the mentally ill was ultimately nothing new or unknown. Rather what one found was the "substrate of our own being," the admittedly enigma-filled substrate of the human unconscious. For Jung, this was an insight that was to become a "powerful emotional experience." Each life story of a patient, laden with portentous signs, led to an adventurous denouement into which he had to place himself.

Early signs of this approach already mark Jung's first psychiatric works, written at Burghölzli. Examples are "The Psychology of Dementia Praecox" and "The Content of the Psychoses," both the fruit of several years of experimental research and clinical observation. Bleuler had every reason to be content with the energy and commitment of his young assistant. For this reason, he persuaded him to undertake an additional semester of study in Paris. There Jung became acquainted with Pierre Janet (1859 – 1947), who was considered the originator of a new system of dynamic psychiatry. He was teaching at Salpêtrière, at the time a psychiatric center of international standing. Freud had also paid a visit there a few years before. Anyone who comes to know Jung's theory of types will encounter traces of Janet's influence. In 1905 Jung became a lecturer at the University of Zurich, and at Burghölzli attained the rank of senior physician. While pursuing his medical practice, he continued lecturing at the university until 1913.

During this period, two events took place without which Jung's subsequent life and work could not have taken the direction they did: a personal encounter with a young Swiss woman from Schaff-

Left: The Burghölzli psychiatric clinic in Zurich (about 1900).

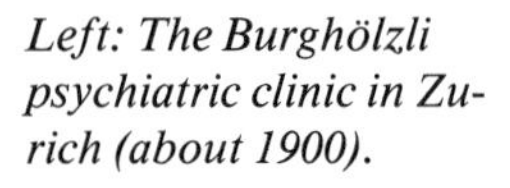

Above right: Wedding portrait (1903).

hausen, Emma Rauschenbach, and another with his mentor and, for a time, friend, Sigmund Freud of Vienna.

Jung had already had occasion to become briefly acquainted with Emma, then a fourteen-year-old girl, at the house of her parents. Although he saw her for only a moment, he knew, "deeply shaken," as he confessed, that he had met his future wife. At the time a penniless and as yet professionless student, he would not have stood a chance of being allowed to court the daughter of a well-to-do manufacturer. But six years later he was already qualified as a doctor and able to ask for Emma Rauschenbach's hand. When in 1902 Jung went to see Janet in Paris, he was already betrothed. On 14 February 1903 the two were married. The couple's first home was in the main building at Burghölzli, one floor above the apartment of Dr. Bleuler. And though it may have appeared that Jung devoted far more time to his work than what was soon to grow into a family, a harmonious partnership was already beginning to develop between him and his wife.

As we know today, it would soon have to survive bitter trials.[18] That this was possible is doubtless to be ascribed to the great personal maturity of Emma Jung-Rauschenbach. For this, there is a good deal of convincing evidence. In addition, over the years Emma developed herself independently as a psychotherapist experienced in both theory and practice. Without Emma Jung as a loving and level-headed life-partner, the life and work of Carl Gustav Jung would have been as impossible as if he had never met and worked with Sigmund Freud.

Following two pages: Paris: street scene around the turn of the century.

Hochzeits-Feier

von

Herrn Dr. med. C. G. Jung

und

Fräulein Emma Rauschenbach

16. Februar 1903.

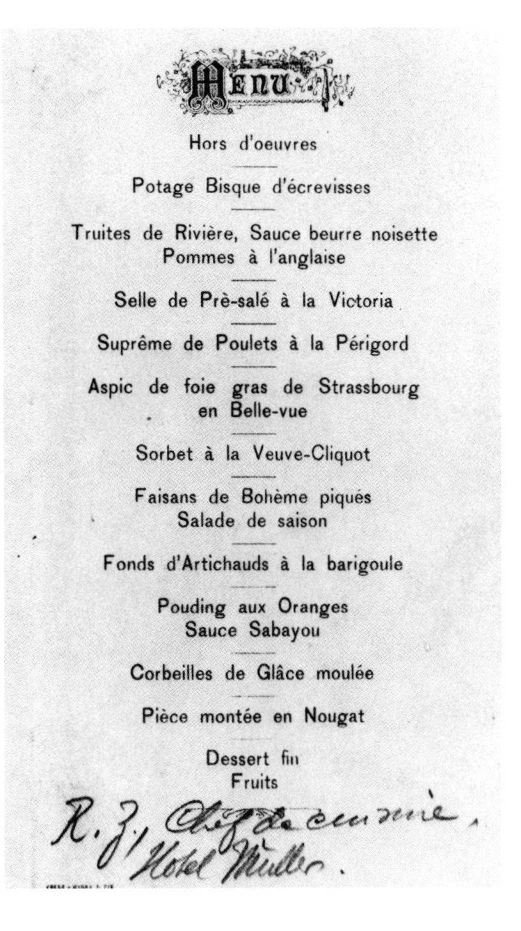

Menu

Hors d'oeuvres

Potage Bisque d'écrevisses

Truites de Rivière, Sauce beurre noisette
Pommes à l'anglaise

Selle de Prè-salé à la Victoria

Suprême de Poulets à la Périgord

Aspic de foie gras de Strassbourg
en Belle-vue

Sorbet à la Veuve-Cliquot

Faisans de Bohème piqués
Salade de saison

Fonds d'Artichauds à la barigoule

Pouding aux Oranges
Sauce Sabayou

Corbeilles de Glâce moulée

Pièce montée en Nougat

Dessert fin
Fruits

Vins

Sherry et Madère
Vin blanc de Meursault 1881
Thaynger Auslese 1900
Forster Jesuitengarten
Château Mouton d'Armaillac 1887
Heidsick Monopol.

Menu and wine list for the wedding reception on February 16, 1903. This shows the upward move in social status the marriage signified for the Swiss parson's son living in modest circumstances.

TRE
DU
DEVILLE

Freud. Traum.

Inhalt.

Disposition: Einleitung.

1. Beispiel der Analyse. Kritiklose Rückverfolgung der Associationen.
   a. manifester Trauminhalt.
   b. latenter " "
2. Eintheilung der Träume.
   a. sinnvoll u. verständlich.
   b. sinnvoll u. unverständlich.
   c. verworren.
3. Kinderträume.
4. Erwachsene. Bequemlichkeitsträume. Wunschträume.
5. Ursachen der Fremdartigkeit des Traumes.
   a. Verdichtung
      α. mittelst des natürl. Gemeinsamen
      β. " einer durch d. Traum selbst geschaffenen Gemeinsamkeit.
   b. Traumverschiebung. Traumentstellung. Entstellung ~~verpönter~~ Gedanken.
   c. anschauliche Darstellung inadequater Vorstellungen. daher Metaphern.
      Sämtliche Metamorphose logischer Nexus.
      ~~Relation~~ Causal: Verwandlung u. bloss Nacheinander.
      Alternativ: = Und.
      Ähnlichkeit, Gemeinsamkeit, Übereinstimmung.
      Widerspruch, Spott, Hohn = Absurdität des manifesten Traumes.
   d. Traumcomposition, zwecks der Verständlichkeit
   e. Darstellung verdrängter Wünsche und Gedanken.
6. Teleologische Auffassung. Traum, der Hüter des Schlafes.

FIRST EXPERIENCE IN DEPTH PSYCHOLOGY

MEETING AND BREAK WITH SIGMUND FREUD

For the foundation of modern depth psychology, the key (and in Jung's judgment "epoch-making") work was Sigmund Freud's *Interpretation of Dreams* (1900). Already the young assistant doctor from Zurich had studied it intensively and was following the researches of his Viennese colleague. Freud was nineteen years his senior and was at the time a quite controversial figure, rejected by the majority of the men in his profession. In the circle of psychiatrists at Burghölzli, with Eugen Bleuler at its head, Jung soon recognized what pioneering scientific work Freud was doing. As late as in his obituary for Freud (1939), decades after the tragic parting of the two men, Jung described Freud's work as "surely the boldest attempt ever made on the apparently solid ground of empiricism to master the riddle of the unconscious psyche. For us young psychiatrists, it was a source of enlightenment, whereas for our older colleagues, it was an object of scorn." In this and other passages something of the enthusiasm and scientific passion that had seized the young psychotherapist comes through.

In July of 1906 Jung composed the foreword to his essay "The Psychology of Dementia Praecox," which appeared in

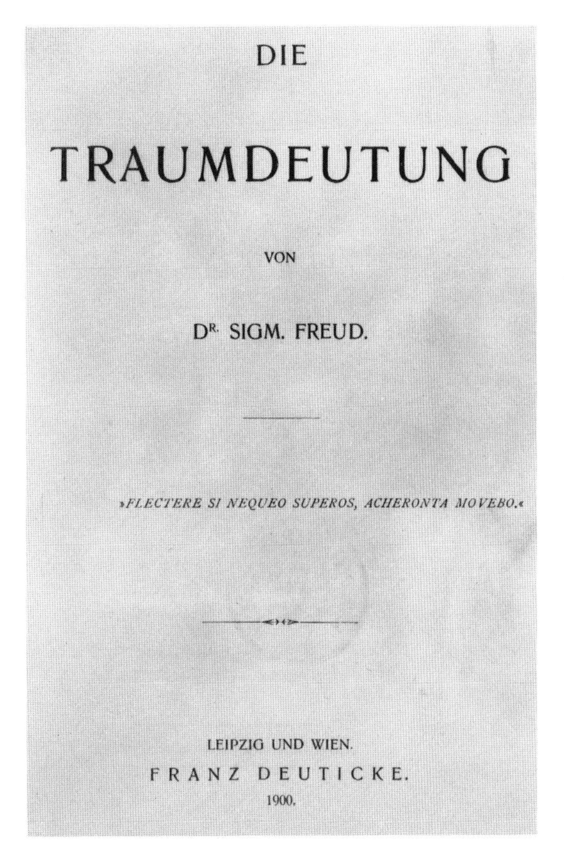

DIE

TRAUMDEUTUNG

VON

DR. SIGM. FREUD.

»FLECTERE SI NEQUEO SUPEROS, ACHERONTA MOVEBO.«

LEIPZIG UND WIEN.
FRANZ DEUTICKE.
1900.

"Justice toward Freud
does not mean, as many fear,
unconditional submission to a dogma.
One can at the same time
quite readily maintain one's
independent point of view."

Sigmund Freud (1856–1939). His work The Interpretation of Dreams *(1900) marked the inception of modern depth psychology.*

Opposite: Jung's handwritten notes on Freud's book The Interpretation of Dreams.

print in the following year. In it the outlines of later ideas – for example, his hypothesis on psychic energy as well as his notion of a collective unconscious with archetypal contents – already were visible. This was about the time that he began his exchange of ideas with Freud by letter.[19] This was soon to be followed by a personal meeting. In this connection, it is instructive to read the assessment of Freud's importance that Jung brought to the situation and to see with what boldness he allied himself with the controversial man:

"Even a superficial glance at the pages of my work will show how much I owe to Freud's ingenious conceptions. ... I can positively say that from the beginning I had all the same objections against Freud that were being raised in the literature. But I said to myself that Freud could be refuted only by someone who himself had frequently employed the psychoanalytic method and who had investigated as Freud had investigated – that is, who had considered daily life, hysteria, and dreams long and patiently from *his* point of view. Someone who had not done this or could not do it had no right to judge Freud; otherwise he would be behaving like those celebrated men of science who had disdained to look through Galileo's telescope."[20]

Jung did not hesitate to commit himself openly to Freud, nor did he hesitate to draw clear distinctions between his position and Freud's. For this reason, it would be inappropriate to characterize Jung as a mere pupil of the Viennese master. For Jung adds:

"Justice toward Freud does not mean, as many fear, unconditional submission to a dogma. One can at the same time quite readily maintain one's independent point of view. For example, if I acknowledge the complex-related mechanisms of dreaming and hysteria, this does not at all mean that I ascribe to infantile sexual trauma the exclusive importance that Freud seems to give it, nor that I place sexuality so predominantly in the foreground or attribute to it the psychological universality that Freud postulates – apparently in response to the powerful role

Vienna around the turn of the century, the first center of psychoanalysis. (From a painting by Franz Alt.)

The university in Zurich (photograph taken in 1905). "In 1905 I became a lecturer in psychiatry and in the same year I became senior physician at the psychiatric clinic of the University of Zurich. I held this position for four years."

that sexuality does undoubtedly play in the psyche."[21]

Jung limits his agreement even more strongly in characterizing the Freudian style of therapy as at best "one of the possible ones." But all in all the basically positive tone during this initial period of the forming psychoanalytic movement is unmistakable. His support of Freud was also given great weight by his critically observing contemporaries. "In Vienna those days ... the prejudice against Freud was so great that it was hard to find a pupil (of his) who still had a reputation to lose," wrote Ernest Jones, Freud's follower and biographer. To this prejudice was added the fact that Freud's first students were almost without exception Jews like himself. Considering the existence of an ever-reawakening anti-Semitism, Freud had to be gravely concerned that psychoanalysis would be misunderstood as purely an internal Jewish affair. Also, apart from the situation in Vienna, the reaction of the psychiatric profession at large was not exactly one of understanding. Jung's call for an objective test was only too apropos. The majority of Freud's colleagues expressed complete disapproval, some going as far as to raise criminal suspicions. As late as 1910 a member of a "secret medical committee" by the name of Weygandt felt it necessary to assert at a physicians' congress in Hamburg that "Freud's theories are of no concern to science, but are rather a matter for the police." His view was that the police should protect decent society from Freud's obscenities.

Jung in his turn also came to feel the opprobrium of his peers. This was of little concern to him, however, because of his inner conviction. "If what Freud says is the truth, then I am on his side. I couldn't care less about a career that requires one to curtail one's research and keep quiet about the truth." Unconcerned about the resistance that was becoming visible, he continued to take Freud's side, even in public discussions at medical congresses. When his *Studies in Word Association* (1905) was published, Jung sent this latest work of his to Vienna. It then emerged that Freud, "out of impatience" as he confessed, had already gotten a hold of the study. He informed his "highly esteemed colleague" in Zurich of this on 11 April 1906. It may be that just before this Eugen Bleuler had been boasting to Freud about his senior physician. In any case, in this way a correspondence began that was to last for several years and number more than 350 letters.[22] In the first seven years, up to 1913, the correspondence was so abundant that hardly a week went by without at least one, often several letters, going back and forth between Vienna and Zurich. Scientific matters were discussed in detail. Personal matters were spoken of with great openness. From October 1908 on, Freud addressed Jung as "dear friend," whereas Jung used the phrase "dear professor." Because the exchange of ideas by correspondence between the two men lasted just seven years and because their paths would soon have to separate, it is worth pointing out that none of Freud's correspondence with any of his other colleagues can be compared to that with Jung – in volume, in human depth, or in power of expression, though he did have significant and instructive exchanges of letters with Bleuler, Binswanger, Pfister, Abraham, Groddeck, Andreas-Salomé, Reik, Reich, Weiss, Putnam, Fe-

A galvanometer, which, among other instruments, Jung used in his early diagnostic studies of association; also some of Jung's own sketches. "In 1904 – 05, I established a laboratory for experimental psychopathology at the psychiatric clinic. There I had a number of students with whom I did research in psychic reactions [i. e., associations] . . . It was also through the associations experiment and the psychogalvanic experiment that I became known in America; soon numerous patients arrived from there."

renczi, Federn, and Rank. Worthy of note in their own right are the few letters from Emma Jung scattered through the collection. Emma wrote not only as a wife, but sometimes very self-confidently supported her husband's position by giving the Viennese master a piece of her mind!

The mutual esteem and friendship grew and developed. Jung never in any way concealed the strong impression Freud had made on him, either in their visits with each other or at congresses of the psychoanalytic movement, where Jung quite soon began to appear as Freud's number-one man, the "crown prince." Still in Jung's memoirs, we find, "Freud was a great man, and what is more, like a man possessed." And again: "Freud was the first man of real importance I had encountered; in my experience up to that time, no else could compare with him. There was nothing the least trivial in his attitude. I found him extremely intelligent, shrewd, and altogether remarkable." But Jung was quick to add: "And yet my first impressions of him remained somewhat tangled; I could not make him out."[23]

Clearly, two elements were mingled in the encounter. On one hand, there was ungrudging recognition of Freud's professional qualities, of his genius and his human greatness; on the other, considerable points of conflict emerged having to do with a variety of things – different personality types as well as different ways of looking at the world. Already, near the beginning of their correspondence, Freud's clairvoyance brought the older man to warn: "Don't distance yourself from me too much when in reality you are so close to me. Otherwise we may yet live to see people playing us off against each other."

Concerning the difference in worldviews, it should be noted with what conviction Freud set himself against what he called the "deluge of black slime, occultism." He hoped to fortify this position with the "bulwark" of his special view on

New York (photograph taken in 1910). After a nine-day sea crossing, the three travelers (Freud, Jung and Ferenczi) arrived in New York on the evening of August 29, 1909. From there, they continued their journey to Boston and Worcester.

the libido. Hence the almost conspiratorial tone: "My dear Jung, promise me never to abandon the sexual theory. That is the most essential thing of all. You see, we must make a dogma of it, an unshakable bulwark." The would-be co-conspirator comments: "This was the thing that struck at the heart of our friendship. I knew I would never be able to accept such an attitude." There is no doubt – as high as the hopes were that Freud set on Jung, the break between them was just as inevitable. But what did Freud mean by "occultism"? It is no secret that genuine esotericism at this point had fallen into disrepute as a result of all manner of obscure fancies. A glance at the relevant literature from the turn of the century is enough to show this clearly. But Jung suspected another reason for Freud's attitude:

"What Freud seemed to mean by "occultism" was virtually everything that philosophy and religion, including the rising contemporary science of parapsychology, had learned about the psyche. To me the sexual theory was just as occult, that is to say, just as unproven an hypothesis, as many other speculative views. As I saw it, a scientific truth was a hypothesis which might be adequate for the moment but was not to be preserved as an article of faith for all time."[24]

Even if we leave completely open the question of the validity of parapsychological research, Freud's views on the subject at the time of his meeting with Jung are not without interest. As might be expected, at that time, around 1909, he completely rejected this entire idea as "nonsense." And Jung, as conciliatory as he tried to be, found it hard not to respond sharply. (Such tact was a virtue, as we often hear, that was not too often at his disposal.)

But now something took place that throws a curious light on the unique relationship of the two men. Jung was visiting Freud in Vienna, at Berggasse 19. In *Memories, Dreams, Reflections,* Jung gives this account of the incident:

"While Freud was going on this way [speaking against parapsychology], I had a curious sensation. It was as if my diaphragm were made of iron and were becoming red-hot – a glowing vault. And at that moment there was such a loud report in the bookcase, which stood right next to us, that we both started up in alarm, fearing the thing was going to topple over on us. I said to Freud: "There, that is an ex-

ample of a so-called catalytic exteriorization phenomenon."

"Oh, come," he exclaimed. "That is sheer bosh."

"It is not," I replied, "You are mistaken Herr Professor. And to prove my point I now predict that in a moment there will be another such loud report!" Sure enough, no sooner had I said the words than the same detonation went off in the bookcase."[25]

Jung had the feeling of having hurt his friend and colleague. The sense of trust that had hitherto reigned seemed to have been subtly disturbed. Both avoided further mention of the Viennese episode in conversation. There is, however, a letter on this subject from Freud to Jung. It is in the appendix to *Memories* and is dated 16 April 1909. In this letter the theme of the "poltergeist," as Freud called it, is taken up once again. We learn here under what circumstances the spontaneous phenomenon had come to pass. The spook appeared in Freud's bookcase "on the same evening that I formally adopted you as an eldest son, anointing you as my successor and crown prince – *in partibus infidelium* – that then and there you should have divested me of my paternal dignity, and that

Below: Main building of Clark University in Worcester (about 1900).

Above: Speakers and guests at the conference of psychologists in September 1909 in Worcester, Massachussetts. C. G. Jung in the front row, third from left, Freud fourth from left.

Küsnacht, d. 30. Oktober 1910.

E. J.

Lieber Herr Professor!
Ich weiss zwar nicht recht, woher ich den Mut nehme, Ihnen diesen Brief zu schreiben, doch glaube ich sicher zu sein, dass es nicht aus Übermut geschieht; sondern ich folge damit der Stimme meines Unbewussten, der ich schon so oft Recht geben musste u. die mich hoffentlich auch diesmal nicht irreführt.

"Do not think of Carl with the sentiments of a father, ... but rather as one man to another." – Emma Jung's letter to Sigmund Freud, October 30, 1910.

the divesting seems to have given you as much pleasure as investing your person gave me."

We see here again, in connection with this, for Freud, enigmatic and uncanny incident, how Freud looked upon his young Swiss colleague, namely, as his spiritual heir who would carry on what he had begun. The ceremonial language he uses – anointing Jung as his crown prince, adopting him as his eldest son – underlines the status that he ascribed to his visitor. This is especially noteworthy when we consider the number of Freud's Viennese pupils, among whom quite a few might hold some claim to his successorship.

Also illuminating is another passage in this same letter in which Freud, with an unmistakable dash of self-directed irony, again conjures up the imaginary father-son relationship with Jung:

"I therefore don once more my horn-rimmed paternal spectacles and warn my dear son to keep a cool head and rather not understand something than make such great sacrifices for the sake of understanding. I also shake my wise gray locks over the question of psychosynthesis and think: Well, that is how the young folks are; they really enjoy things only when they need not drag us along with them, where with our short breath and weary legs we cannot follow."

Freud wrote these sentences in his fifty-third year.

Now how did Jung react to this kind of allusion? As the now completely edited version of the correspondence makes clear, and as the elderly Jung confirmed in his memoirs, he regarded his relationship with Freud as "extremely valuable." "I experienced Freud as being the older, more mature, and more experienced person and myself as like his son."

This testimony is one we must respect. On the other hand, Jung's English friend and colleague E. A. Bennet was clearly justified in stressing that there was nothing between Freud and Jung in the strict sense of what we think of as the master-pupil relationship. We should also not disregard the comments of others who were close to the relationship. Such a view also emerges clearly from the correspondence, as well as from the fact that Freud honored Jung above his long-time followers by delegating teaching and leadership tasks to him.

This preferential treatment is further underlined by the fact that Jung was invited with Freud in 1909 to lecture at Clark University in Worcester, Massachusetts. This trip, on which they were accompanied by Freud's follower Ferenczi, lasted seven weeks and made it possible for the two men to spend time together daily.

The trip to America proved a total success for both men. Jung's tremendous gre-

Group photograph from the Third International Psychoanalytic Congress, which took place on September 21 and 22, 1911, in Weimar, Germany. Emma Jung (first row, third from right) participated not only as her husband's wife but also as his colleague.

gariousness brought a further result. His lectures were translated into English by Abraham A. Brill and published in professional journals. In this way, he made a significant contribution to psychoanalysis' gaining a foothold in the new world. Already in 1911 the American Psychoanalytic Association was formed, with James J. Putnam as president and Ernest Jones as secretary. As might be expected, Jung's work had quite a positive effect on the spread of psychoanalysis. And it may have been clear only for a few adepts that his emphasis was different from Freud's. Out of consideration for their hosts and for those still to be won over to the new psychoanalytic approach, care was taken to keep the already existing divergences out of the public light. This went especially for the divergent views concerning sexuality. All the same, Jung emphasized the importance for him of the archetypal structural elements of the psyche, that is, just those factors that point beyond the individual psyche. Then, he pointed out, if one wants to understand the manifestations of this transpersonal collective unconscious as they appear, for example, in dreams, working with mythology becomes ever more necessary. Even Freud did not fail to be impressed by this, as can be learned from the correspondence of these years.

It was not only with an honorary doctorate (Doctor of Laws *honoris causa*) that Jung returned to Switzerland from the United States, but also with the knowledge that the genius of Freud, viewed by him under the influence of a father projection, appeared to exhibit considerable defects.

In the context of their intensive conversations and the analyses they undertook together in the course of the long sea-crossings, it could no longer remain hidden from him that Freud placed "personal authority before the truth." In his memoirs, Jung gives detailed accounts of this. Such observations or interpretations, however, continued to be pushed into the background by the possibility of intensive collaboration in person and in writing.

"The rest is silence." This letter from Jung (January 6, 1913) marks the definitive break with Freud. The official and distant tone is underlined still further by the letterhead "International Psychoanalytic Association."

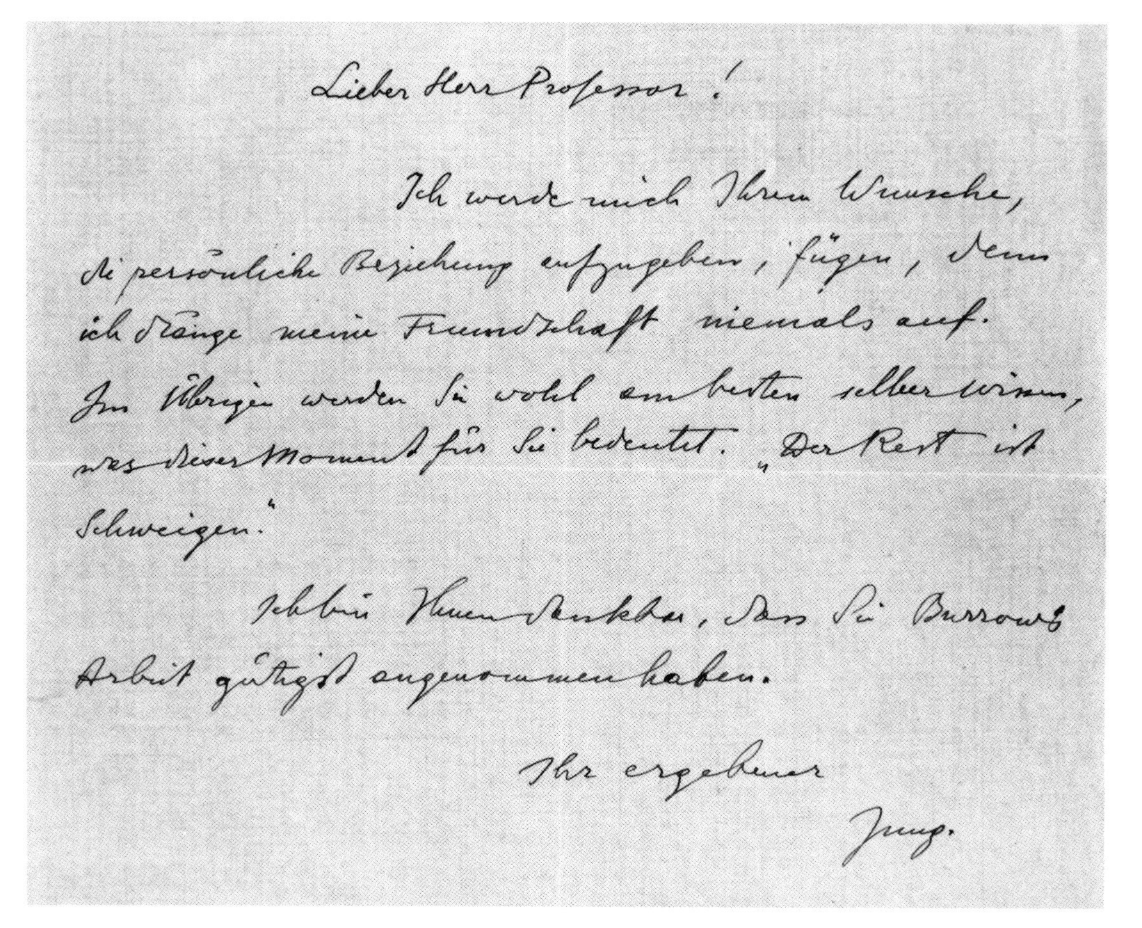

Lieber Herr Professor!

Ich werde mich Ihrem Wunsche, die persönliche Beziehung aufzugeben, fügen, denn ich dränge meine Freundschaft niemals auf. Im Übrigen werden Sie wohl am besten selber wissen, was dieser Moment für Sie bedeutet. „Der Rest ist Schweigen."

Ich bin Ihnen dankbar, dass Sie Burrow's Arbeit gütigst angenommen haben.

Ihr ergebener

Jung.

C. G. Jung about 1905.

Occasions for this were provided by annual congresses and by Jung's administrative participation in the publication of the psychoanalytic journals that were gradually creating wider acceptance for psychoanalysis. If one looks at the group photograph from the congress at Weimar (1911), it is evident even visually how Freud and Jung formed the pulsating nucleus of the entire movement. The work of their colleagues fell into place in relation to the psychological force field that they generated.

What was it then actually that led to the break between Sigmund Freud and C. G. Jung? This question cannot be answered in a few sentences. As already indicated, several factors were at work. That Jung and Freud had arrived at quite different views is clear. Moreover, we would not go awry by saying that the meeting of the two men represented a very fateful episode in Jung's development. Freud, with his scientific achievement and personality, was for Jung only a kind of way station. A lifelong collaboration between the two men, if only because of their differing worldviews and psychological premises, was out of the question.

There was also another factor, which Jung saw in the following terms. "Freud himself had a neurosis, no doubt diagnosable and one with highly troublesome symptoms, as I had discovered on our trip to America. ... Apparently neither Freud nor his disciples could understand what it meant for the theory and practice of psychoanalysis if not even the master could deal with his own neurosis." The absolute status Freud and his followers attributed to the psychoanalytic method and Freud's well-nigh dogmatic theory was obviously the decisive point in Jung's decision to put an end to their collaboration. He had no other choice but to withdraw from the relationship, especially when he learned that Freud doubted his integrity. "Since this is the gravest accusation that one can make against a man, you have made it impossible for me to work together with you further," we read in Jung's letter of 27 October 1913.[26] This was his declaration of a definitive break. It came after Freud had already suggested, at the beginning of that year, "that we give up our private relationship altogether. I lose nothing by this, since emotionally, for a long time already, I have been bound to you only by the thin thread of the after-effect of previously experienced disappointments. ... Assume complete freedom and spare me the supposed 'duties of friendship.'"

"The rest is silence," is the phrase that Jung used in his answering letter.[27] At this point also the local Zurich chapter of the Psychoanalytic Association, hitherto much valued by Freud, withdrew from the organization. (Eugen Bleuler, the chapter's head, also distanced himself from Jung at this point, though for other reasons.)

Both men suffered greatly from the failure of their relationship. A classical formula that Freud resorted to immediately after the break could not hide this fact. At the end of July 1913 he wrote, "So we are finally rid of them – brutish Saint Jung and his henchmen in prayer."[28] When the American doctor E. A. Bennet visited the seventy-two-year-old at his Vienna home in 1932 and asked him how it had been for him when Alfred Adler and C. G. Jung had left him, Freud replied that Adler's departure had not been a loss over which he had to mourn, but "Jung was a great loss." This is one of Freud's very few retrospective comments about Jung. Jung himself behaved quite differently in this regard. Up till the end of his life, he reaffirmed on many occasions his early opinion of Freud. On March 29, 1949 he wrote to the son of his friend Theodore Flournoy that Freud's was "the honour of having discovered the first archetype, the Oedipus complex. That is a mythological and a psychological motif simultaneously." And in a letter written in April 1957 to a German physician, he stated:

19 Berggasse in Vienna's ninth district, the site of Freud's apartment and office between 1891 and 1938. Here also the meetings between Freud and Jung took place.

"Despite the resounding censure I suffered at the hands of Freud, I cannot, even despite my resentment toward him, fail to recognize his importance as a critical analyst of culture and as a pioneer in the field of psychology. A true evaluation of Freud's endeavors extends into domains that concern not only Jews but Europeans altogether, domains that I tried to illuminate through my work. Without Freud's "psychoanalysis," the key would have been entirely missing for me."[29]

The Jung family house in Küsnacht on Lake Zurich. "At that time [in early childhood], the idea became firmly established in me that I must live by a lake. Without water, so I thought, one could not exist at all."

Personal Crisis and Emergence of His Work

Looking at the years immediately following the separation from Freud, it is clear that this break also meant a deep and fateful gap in Jung's personal life. This can be seen in several different perspectives.

Externally, Jung remained the reputable physician, who, after his trip to America and a number of foreign lecture tours, had a distinguished international clientele. But the years following Jung's separation from the Psychoanalytic Association were no mere continuation of the preceding ones. Jung resigned from his position as lecturer in the medical faculty of the university, naturally without abandoning his scientific work. On the contrary, a new phase in his work was about to begin. The signal for this, in the form of the publication of an important book, had already sounded. This book, *Wandlungen und Symbole der Libido* (Transformation and Symbols of the Libido), had appeared shortly before the separation from Freud – part in 1911, part in 1912 – in the *Jahrbuch für Psychoanalytische und Psychopathologische Forschungen* (Annual Journal for Psychoanalytic and Psychopathological Research). It was a formulation of Jung's position that formed a basis for the development of his future work. Jung recounts what he experienced at this time in a foreword to the significantly altered new version of the work, which appeared much later under the present title of *Symbols of Transformation* (1952): "I had to gather my material where I found it. There was no possibility of letting my ideas ripen. The whole thing came over me like an avalanche that cannot be held back. ... It was the explosion of all those contents of the psyche that had no place in the stifling narrowness of the Freudian psychology and worldview." Nevertheless, the author retrospectively referred to this work as a "milestone." Indeed this book, which places so much importance on the (superpersonal) mythos in its meaning for the life of the individual psyche, was to become the "program for the ensuing decades" of Jung's life and work. For, as mentioned at the start:

"The psyche is not of the present. Its age is to be counted in the millions of years. The individual consciousness is only the flower and fruit of a season that grows out of the perennial rhizome under the earth, and it finds itself better attuned to the truth when it takes the existence of the rhizome into account, for the root system is the mother of all."[30]

Here Jung expresses one of his primary goals – to free medical psychology from the "reductive causalism" of classical psychoanalysis and to show that the unconscious extends far beyond the sphere of the individual. Implicit also is the idea that not only is the psyche connected to a psychic past, but everything having to do with the psyche possesses an unmistakable goal orientation (teleology) that must be taken into account in therapy.

At this point we must clearly distinguish between merely going along with a given state of affairs intellectually and, beyond that, finding a way to enter into it experientially. This is the very distinction that characterizes the basis and origin of C. G. Jung's analytical psychology as a whole. This becomes clear if we look closely at Jung's historical circumstances in relation to the circumstances of his own life. In the middle period of his life, often a time of crisis requiring an existential turnabout, Jung found himself in the midst of the critical developments in European history that ultimately led to the outbreak of the First World War in 1914. How intensively the collective plight of the nations was unconsciously preoccupying Jung can be seen from an imaginary image that came to him in October 1913, which he described as a "vision" somewhat in the sense of the visions of the Old Testament prophets:

"I saw a monstrous flood covering all the northern and low-lying lands between

Dem Lehrer und Meister zu Füssen gelegt von einem ungehorsamen aber dankbaren Schüler.

WANDLUNGEN UND SYMBOLE DER LIBIDO.

BEITRÄGE ZUR ENTWICKLUNGSGESCHICHTE DES DENKENS.

VON

DR. MED. ET JUR. C. G. JUNG,

PRIVATDOZENT DER PSYCHIATRIE AN DER UNIVERSITÄT IN ZÜRICH.

SONDERABDRUCK AUS DEM JAHRBUCH FÜR PSYCHOANALYTISCHE UND PSYCHOPATHOLOGISCHE FORSCHUNGEN, III. UND IV. BAND.

LEIPZIG UND WIEN.
FRANZ DEUTICKE.
1912.

The early work Transformations and Symbols of the Libido *(1912) on the one hand marked the separation between Jung and Freud, and on the other hand opened new perspectives on Jung's future path as an investigator of the psyche.*

the North Sea and the Alps. When it came up to Switzerland I saw that the mountains grew higher and higher to protect our country. I realized that a frightful catastrophe was in progress. I saw the mighty yellow waves, the floating rubble of civilization, and the drowned bodies of uncounted thousands. Then the whole sea turned to blood."[31]

Only ten months later this horrendous vision began turning into a reality. But Jung also had dreams of confidence, such as the one that in spite of a worldwide cold spell grapes were ripening, yielding a healing juice. "I plucked the grapes and gave them to the waiting crowd." That psychotherapeutic knowledge when administered properly in the right dosage can become healing medicine is self-evident. But before this could happen, the would-be therapist had to come to terms himself with the powers of sickness and the psychic danger posed by it. He had to dare to confront the psychic potencies

"The whole thing came over me like an avalanche that cannot be held back ... It was the explosion of all those contents of the psyche that there was no place for in the stifling narrowness of the Freudian psychology and worldview."

that can drive one to the edge of the abyss of total psychic dissociation, madness. He had to work with fantasies filled with mythological images and with sensations laden with emotions of all kinds. Now and again, eruptions from the unconscious threatened to overwhelm his consciousness. And as a clinically experienced psychologist, it was clear to him what depths threatened him if he failed to regain and stabilize his psychological balance, whether by painstaking self-anamnesis, playful creative activity, yoga exercises, or other means. Jung described his psychological state with merciless candor:

"The unconscious contents could have driven me out of my wits. But my family and the knowledge: I have a medical diploma from a Swiss university, I must help my patients, I have a wife and five children, I live at 228 Seestrasse in Küsnacht – these were actualities which made demands upon me and proved to me again and again that I really existed, that I was not a blank page whirling about in the winds of the spirit, like Nietzsche. Nietzsche had lost the ground under his feet because he possessed nothing more than the inner world of his thoughts – which incidentally possessed him more than he it. He was uprooted and suspended above the earth, and therefore he succumbed to exaggeration and irreality. For me, such irreality was the quintessence of horror, for I aimed, after all, at this world and *this* life.[32]

A strong sense of the affirmation of life is eloquently expressed in Jung's whole life story. All those who met him and shared his life have borne witness to this. Thus even in these critical years he, who had literally "built on the water," did not give up his favorite sport, sailing. Surely water, as an image, is an expression of the tides of the unconscious, with its depths and shoals, its play of waves, and its rolling surf. To this can be added the archetypal-mythological significance of seafaring. Thus at one point, like a man challenging the power of the elements, he sailed back and forth across Lake Zurich for four days. In his mind was the image of Odysseus' adventurous sea journey by night *(nekyia)*. His childhood friend Albert Oeri and three younger companions made up the complement of the company, as it were, of the Odysseus of Lake Zurich. Did they have any notion of what was going on within Jung? He had Oeri read aloud the highly suggestive nekyia episode from Homer's Odyssey. This is the account of a journey to the eerie mythical shores of the realm of shadows

Opposite: The sacred, at once flaming and order-producing, above the world of technology and war. This image, rendered in 1920, is derived from a dream of January 22, 1914.

The so-called Red Book, a volume bound in red leather, that preserves Jung's experiences in words and images.

"In the Red Book
I tried an esthetic
elaboration of my fantasies,
but never finished it.
I became aware
that I had not yet found
the right language
that I had
still to translate it
into something else."

German soldiers, enthusiastic for war, just after the outbreak of the First World War, on their way to the French front . . .

. . . and the reality – burnt earth, millions of dead.

and to the abode of the departed. In it, Homer's hero recounts to the listening Phaeacians:

"The sun was sinking into the sea as we, driven on by a wondrous wind in our sails, arrived at the end of the world on the shores of the Cimmerians, which lie in eternal mist, never illuminated by the beams of the sun, beside the stream of Ocean, which girdles the world. We came to the rock and the confluence of the rivers of the dead that Circe had told us of, and we made offering precisely according to her instructions. (*Odyssey,* 11)"

Such texts contain a special meaningfulness, an almost incantatory impact, for someone who must undergo the nocturnal sea journey of the soul. By this time Jung was already certain, and became increasingly certain, that it was necessary for him to undergo this primordial experience himself in order to be able, as one who has gone through it, to bring the light of understanding to the existential darkness of his patients. Otherwise, he could not have written: "I have never distanced myself from my early experiences. All my work, everything I have accomplished intellectually, has come out of my first imaginations and dreams." Such testimony, today as earlier, cannot be taken seriously enough in studying the literary works of C. G. Jung. He was aware in those critical months, that he was struggling with the "building blocks of a psychosis." The psychiatrist knew what kind of peril he was talking about. . . .

From the torrent within him, teeming with fantasies and imaginations from his unconscious, from time to time images arose like those familiar from mythology or the works of the gnostics of the ancient world, for example, Basilides, a major heretical figure of the second century C. E. Then also a certain Philemon made himself known, a wisdom figure, who provided Jung with inspirations that he afterwards retained. A host of ghostlike figures made its presence felt; in fact there were ghostlike manifestations that were perceived even by Jung's disturbed family. Although after a time a process of clarification and brightening of his state of mind took place, it nevertheless was several decades before Jung was able to convert what he had experienced between 1912 and 1919 into psychological knowledge concerning the archetypal nature of reality and give it form in his work and writings. Only the reader who has looked into the biographical background from which these writings arose can have an idea of their implications. Careful study

shows that the factors that touched his life are the same ones that are significant for the development of his work.

Thus, one day when he was flooded with images that gave him the feeling of being in a "land of the dead," he glimpsed two human figures – an old man and a beautiful young woman – standing at the foot of a cliff. Mustering all his courage and resolve, he approached them in order to discover their meaning. He had the feeling that he was confronting real people. He recounts that he "listened attentively to what they told me. The old man explained that he was Elijah, and that gave me a shock. But the girl staggered me even more, for she called herself Salome! She was blind. What a strange couple: Salome and Elijah. But Elijah assured me that he and Salome had belonged together from all eternity, which completely astounded me. ... They had a black serpent living with them which displayed an unmistakable fondness for me. I stuck close to Elijah because he seemed to be the most reasonable of the three, and to have a clear intelligence. Of Salome I was distinctly suspicious. Elijah and I had a long conversation which, however, I did not understand. Naturally I tried to find a plausible explanation for the appearance of Biblical figures in my fantasy by reminding myself that my father had been a clergyman. But that really explained nothing at all. For what did the old man signify? What did Salome signify? Why were they together?"[33]

For the psychologist, there was no doubt about what he had to comprehend in this scene. In one way or another, these figures must have to do with himself; simply put, they must be partial aspects of his psyche. He sought to apply his knowledge of mythological themes, as well as themes from the ancient mysteries, among which early Christian gnosticism can be reckoned, in interpreting these creations of his own psyche. In brief, he tried to explain similar motifs in terms of each other. Today in analytical psychology, we speak of "amplification," that is, the enriching of imaginary or dreamed images through related motifs from religious or

"In 1918 – 19, I was commander of the English region of prisoners of war at Château d'Œx."

Above and below: English prisoners of war.

Middle: Jung (first from left) as a medical corps officer, along with English and French officers.

Philemon and other figures, drawn by Jung about 1917.

"Philemon and other fantasy figures brought me the decisive knowledge that there are things in the psyche that I do not produce, but that produce themselves and have their own life."

intellectual history or from myths or fairy tales. In accordance with this approach, in our case not only Elijah but also Salome could be connected with the masculine psyche. By using the method of amplification, Jung later arrived, for example, at the concept of the so-called soul image. In a man it usually manifests as a feminine figure. This is the anima. A woman also produces or imagines a figure of the opposite sex, the animus. These terms refer to two typical, or more precisely, archetypal – primally symbolic – formations of the unconscious, which, by definition, we do not perceive consciously. Jung's interpretation of his own vision was as follows:

"Salome is an anima figure. She is blind because she does not see the meaning of things. Elijah is the figure of the wise old prophet and represents the factor of intelligence and knowledge; Salome, the erotic element. One might say that the two figures are personifications of Logos and Eros."[34]

But this explanation does not yet say anything about the actual functional significance of these figures, nor anything about the role of the soul image in Jungian depth psychology. Here we are doing no more than showing how very much the major elements of Jung's theory stem from an actual *theoria,* that is, an inner vision, and cannot be derived from a mere series of rational deductions. In this sense, Jung is an empiricist, and this is how he saw himself his whole life long. But it was only in the process of forming his complete theory or teaching, which had to stand up to the test of dream interpretation and practical psychotherapy, that such details begin to fit together like tiles in a mosaic. And there is another insight that the creator of analytical psychology gained during these years of struggle with his own unconscious, namely, that it is helpful and also therapeutic to give such dreams and fantasies a definite external form. This can be done through written notes, or by drawing, painting, or through some other creative process. This is what he did himself. Today in art therapy and creativity therapy, which are drawing ever increasing interest, these insights are still

showing their practical value. A part of his notes at this time were written by Jung in his so-called Black Book. Aniela Jaffé described this as a series of six small volumes bound in black leather. These accounts of Jung's period of crisis took their final form in the Red Book, a volume that must be considered as having the character of an intimate journal, not intended for publication. In it, Jung used a calligraphic script and put in many large color illustrations of his inner visions. Jung explained in his memoirs:

"In the Red Book I tried an esthetic elaboration of my fantasies, but never finished it. I became aware that I had not yet found the right language, that I still had to translate it into something else. Therefore I gave up this estheticizing tendency in good time, in favor of a rigorous process of understanding. I saw that so much fantasy needed firm ground underfoot, and that I must first return wholly to reality. For me, reality meant scientific comprehension. I had to draw concrete conclusions from the insights the unconscious had given me – and that task was to become a life work."[35]

In concrete terms this meant that Jung had to present his relationship with the unconscious, the inner dialogue with the anima (Salome) and with the old wise man (Elijah or Philemon), in such a way that individual experience could be comprehended in general terms and evaluated by others.

This painting by Jung was done around 1903. "Below the harbor, over the sea wall the deep blue sea, and in the harbor, the sailboat with the two lateen sails that I once painted." (Jung in a letter to his wife from Sousse, Tunisia, March 15, 1920.)

A page of text from the book Septem Sermones ad Mortuos *("Seven Sermons to the Dead"), in which Jung, inspired by Gnostic traditions, presented his inner experiences in didactic-poetic language. (See* Memories, Dreams, Reflections, *1963, pp. 378–90.)*

Opposite: C. G. Jung about 1920, around the time when he was writing Psychological Types.

SERMO IV

XVII

ie toten füllten murrend den raum und ſprachen:

Rede zu uns von Göttern und Teufeln, verfluchter.

Gott Sonne iſt das höchſte gut, der Teufel das gegenteil, alſo habt ihr zwei götter.
Es giebt aber viele hohe güter und viele ſchwere uebel, und darunter giebt es zwei gottteufel, der eine iſt das BRENNENDE und der andere das WACHSENDE.

Das Brennende iſt der EROS in geſtalt der flamme. Sie leuchtet, indem ſie verzehrt.
Das Wachſende iſt der BAUM DES LEBENS, er grünt, indem er wachſend lebendigen ſtoff anhäuft.
Der Eros flammt auf und ſtirbt dahin, der Lebensbaum aber wächſt langſam und ſtätig durch ungemeſſene zeiten.
Gutes und uebles einigt ſich in der flamme.
Gutes und uebles einigt ſich im wachstum des baumes
Leben und liebe ſtehen in ihrer göttlichkeit gegeneinander.

Unermeßlich, wie das heer der ſterne iſt die zahl der götter und teufel.
Jeder ſtern iſt ein gott und jeder raum, den ein ſtern füllt, iſt ein teufel. Das leervolle des ganzen aber iſt das Pleroma.
Die wirkung des ganzen iſt der Abraxas, nur unwirkliches ſteht ihm entgegen.

LAYING THE FOUNDATIONS OF ANALYTICAL PSYCHOLOGY

A FRESH BURST OF CREATIVITY

Jung came out of the period of the "nocturnal sea journey" of the soul as a man ready for further creation. It is not surprising that in the period after publication of the direction-setting *Wandlungen und Symbole der Libido* few new publications of his appeared. A number of years would pass before the investigator of the psyche would appear before the public again as an author. It had to be shown to what extent the analytical psychology he had inaugurated differed from the psychoanalysis of Sigmund Freud. Especially, it had to be shown to what extent Jung's work represented a broadening of intellectual and psychic horizons. Merely making such claims would be ineffective. The process of substantiating them and formulating them would require much time.

From anyone exploring new territories in what Heraclitus called "the immeasurable domain of the psyche," one cannot expect "final" research results. This lies in the very nature and capacity for change of the human psyche. In formulating theories of depth psychology, new continents continue to appear on the horizon and must be accounted for. Especially in this realm, the process of conveying knowledge remains in flux. Jung's

"This is the first mandala I constructed in the year 1916, wholly unconscious of what it meant."

psychological utterances sometimes lack a certain solidity, an easily grasped unequivocal quality common to scientific descriptions of fact. Jung once expressed the problem as follows: "New ideas that do not simply carry us away usually require at least a generation to take hold, and innovations in psychology take quite a bit longer, because especially in this area everybody presents himself as an authority."

Thus it took a fairly long time for Jung to hand over to the printer the major works for which he is known today, starting with *Psychological Types* (1921) and continuing on to the mature work of his later years, *Mysterium Coniunctionis* (1955/56). A shorter work, which was nevertheless important for the continuation of his practical psychotherapeutic activity, was his piece published in 1916 on the so-called transcendental functions. The importance of this work lies in the fact that here for the first time he refers to the active imagination methodology he had developed. In this work we find the first expression of his latest discoveries in working with his own unconscious. For in active imagination, while remaining completely without preconceptions, one lets the spontaneously arisen figures of a given fantasy or dream, whether they are humans or animals, speak to one. One also asks them questions and then, without any intentional manipulation, waits for an "answer." (Of course practical application of this method requires psychotherapeutic guidance – it should not be attempted frivolously.)[36]

There is no better example of the potentiality for, and need of, development in Jung's work than his "On the Psychology of the Unconscious," which came out under various titles between 1912 and 1942. The repeated changes of title reflect the author's need to rework his earlier material. Thus it does not work here, as it sometimes does, to try to glimpse an author's final views in the first versions of his texts.[37] These changes are not least the result of the fluctuations of the psyche itself, as Jung experienced them in his own case. In the foreword to the second edition of the book in the closing year of the First World War (1918), that is, after Jung had for the most part passed through his years of crisis, we read:

"Still too few look inward into their own selves and still too few pose to themselves the question of whether human society would not ultimately be best served by each person beginning with himself in throwing off the old order, by testing out those laws and triumphs that he

Jung repeatedly indicated that mandala drawings have an integrative and thus therapeutic effect only if they arise spontaneously, that is, are not merely mimicked. These mandala drawings, done in the late thirties, are those of a female patient.

Opposite page: Gnostic intaglios. Jung was occupied with these principally in the twenties, before he turned his attention to alchemy. Related style elements appear in his first mandala (see p. 50).

preaches on every streetcorner first on himself alone, on his own person and on his own inner state, rather than pressing them on his fellow men."[38]

Now, in order to achieve a better understanding of his own enigma-laden self with its mysterious modes of expression, and in order to better decipher its messages, it was necessary to gain support from relevant bodies of knowledge. Sigmund Freud had already realized the importance of mythology in this regard. He knew how fruitful it could be for psychotherapy, even though the styles of interpretation might take many different directions. Looking beyond this, Jung began to search for, what he called "prefigurations" – forms that had been elaborated in the past that would be suitable for purposes of comparison in the work of interpreting the manifestations of the psyche. Even before 1920 he had come upon the early Christian gnostics, who knew something of the structure of opposites in the mind, of the polarity between light and darkness, the spiritual and the material, the masculine and the feminine. The poles require each other so as to be able to constellate or enact wholeness as the *mysterium coniunctionis,* as the mystery of the union of opposites, as the essential expression of the "sacred marriage."[39] Even though his occupation with gnostic ideas lasted for only a few years, because the psychological and historical gap between gnosticism and contemporary experience proved to be fairly great, the gnostic texts and related imagic material nevertheless provided a starting point. With their help, he was nevertheless able to begin working on inner experiences through words and images. "Very gradually the outlines of an inner change began making their appearance within me. In 1916 I felt an urge to give shape to something. I was compelled from within, as it were, to formulate and express what might have been said by Philemon." As a first summing up, Jung wrote *Septem Sermones ad Mortuos* (The Seven Sermons to the Dead), "written by Basilides in Alexandria, the City where the East Toucheth the West."[40] Here east and west refer not to external geographical regions but to the inner hemispheres of the conscious and the unconscious. Thus Sermon 1 begins: "The dead came back from Jerusalem,

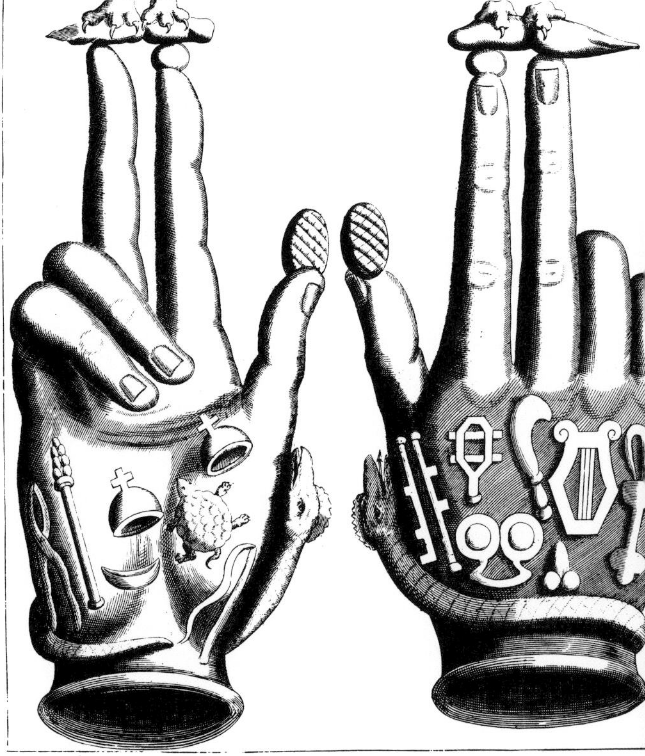

This page: Alchemical-hermetic symbolic drawings.

where they found not what they sought. They prayed me let them in and besought my word, and thus I began my teaching."

The writings of the fictitious gnostic Basilides are still entirely immersed in the realm of the imagination; they are like first hints or adumbrations of material that still had to be converted into the conceptual language of daytime consciousness.

The first mandala (from Sanskrit, "circle") created by Jung, also embellished with mythological imagery, arose at this time as well. In it also the opposites of above and below, right and left, inside

and outside, are unified into an integral structure, likewise an expression of the Self that is not to be confused with man's empirical ego. It is not difficult to see why Jung became so fascinated by the structure of the circle. A mandala is the embodiment of a human symbol that appears in the East as well as the West, ultimately because it is an archetypal manifestation.

Mandala drawings go back many thousands of years to a time in which the wheel as such had not yet been discovered. Circular scratchings in rock have been estimated to be twenty thousand years old. Since that time, as can be documented, the symbol of the circle has had a dominant place in human consciousness.

The mandala is indigenous to the spiritual and religious world of the East, to Tibetan Buddhism and tantric yoga. It is partly a representation of the outer, partly of the inner, cosmos. Thus it is understandable that it is used as an aid to meditation. In this connection, it requires no special exposition to show that the man-

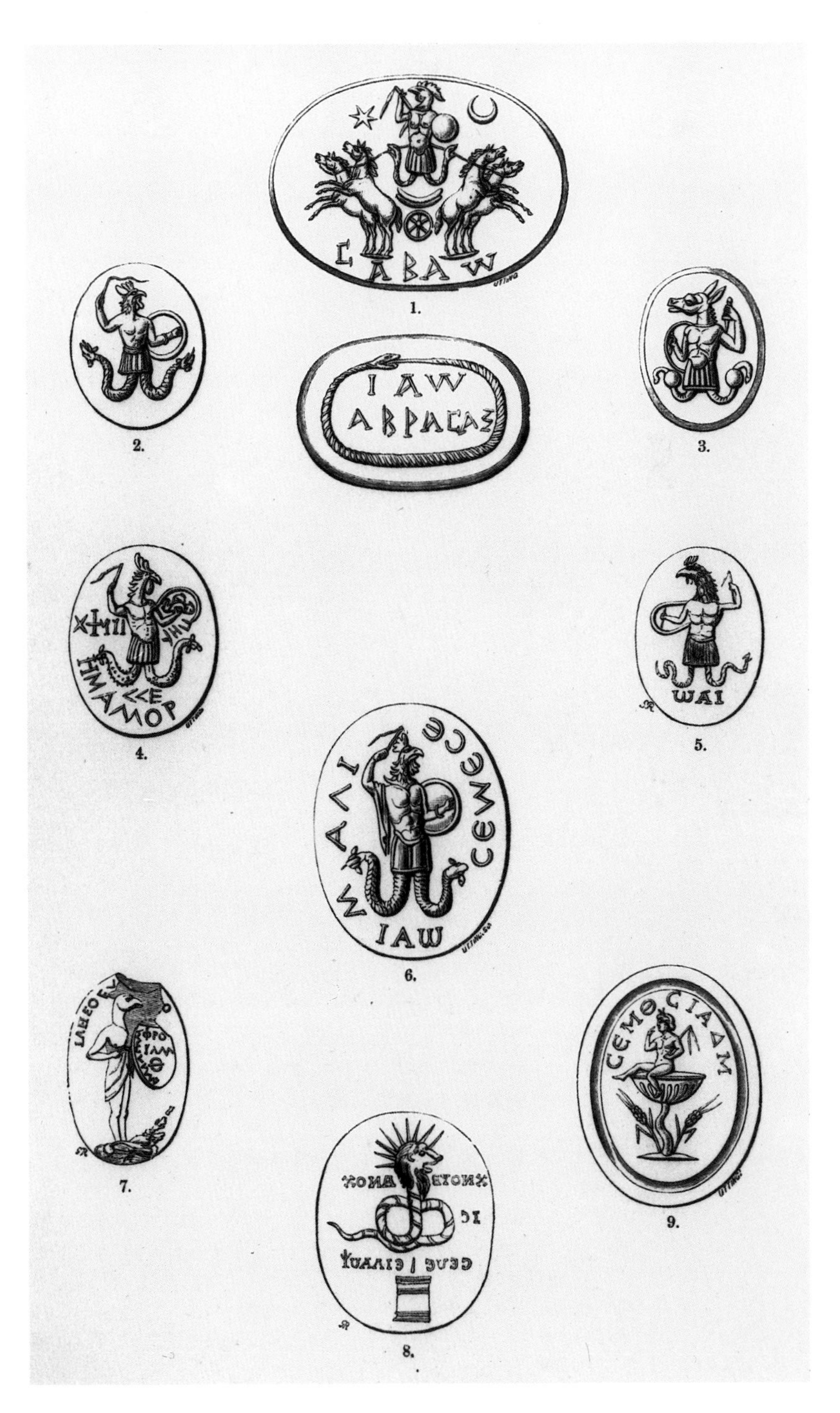

dala determines the structure of all sacred buildings, not least in Christianity. We need only think of the countless representations of Christ enshrined in the apses of churches, the Christ monogram in its manifold forms, or the artistically constructed rose windows of medieval cathedrals.

What does all this mean for a depth psychology, the function of which is to restore unwholesome tendencies of disharmony and dissociation to a framework of order and balance? Again and again Jung sketched the beginnings of an answer to this, in connection with his studies of the symbology of the mandala as well as in connection with alchemical ideas:

"Things that reach as far back in human history as the mandala does of course touch upon the deepest layer of the unconscious and are capable of grasping it where conscious language proves entirely impotent. Such things are not to be thought of conceptually, but must once again grow forth from the obscure depths of oblivion in order to express the uttermost idea of consciousness and the highest intuition of the spirit, and thus fuse the uniqueness of the consciousness of the present with the primordial past of life.[41]

But to reach these insights, which had to prove themselves again and again in the course of his medical practice, Jung had to travel a long road. We know that in the time during the First World War, from 1916 to 1918, when he worked in an internment camp for Englishmen, he drew a mandala every morning. On the one hand, it seemed to reflect his momentary psychological state; on the other, it was part of his unique way of working on the productions of the unconscious. The goal of this work, its actual significance – so he gradually learned – is self-realization, *individuation,* in turn an expression of a single great life-encompassing process of integration, which usually enters a crucial phase in the middle period of life.

A glance at the 1920s, however, shows that Jung first had to come to terms with other themes, themes that seemed to be more accessible to the general consciousness. Among these were the classification of human character types – our typical approach to ourselves and the world around us. Connected with this was the question of what function a dominant role and a less dominant role had. Moreover, he felt the need to see other psychic landscapes in situ. This would take the form of various journeys.

"One does not become enlightened by imagining figures of light, but by making the darkness conscious." Here, the encounter with the shadow within psychic processes – a drawing from the "Red Book."

Opposite: The Buddhist Wheel of Life.

Ernst Kretschmer (1888 – 1964), author of the typology Körperbau und Character *("Physique and Character").*

Opposite: The attempt to classify human character types is immemorial. Here is an illustration from Johann Georg Gichtel's Kurze Eröffnung und Anweisung der drei Prinzipien *("Concise Exposition and Instruction Concerning the Three Principles", 1779). This representation is based on the three-principles doctrine of Jakob Böhme (1575 – 1624). It is primarily intended to lead to a spiritual knowledge of self, world, and God.*

Investigation of Psychological Types

Can people be classified according to personality types? There are numerous methods that try to determine such classifications, varying according to the Psychological orientation. Yet there is widespread agreement that no typology can grasp the unique and individuality of each person. Nonetheless, there has been no dearth of attempts in the course of the past thousands of years to reduce the bodily, psychological and spiritual aspects of the human makeup to common denominators.

Forerunners in this respect were the early Greek thinkers and physicians. Each in his own way made a contribution to the solution of this problem. The basic outlook of each thinker was the key factor determining his view of man and the world. The best known is the classification into four temperaments: sanguine, choleric, phlegmatic, and melancholic. Empedocles associated them with the four elements; Hippocrates, with the four humors; and Aristotle, with the four properties of the blood. In addition to these ancient temperament types, modern psychology has developed a rich assortment of typologies.

C. G. Jung published his *Psychological Types* in 1921. It is the first major work he produced after his separation from Freud. Curiously, two other typologies appeared in the same year: that of Hermann Rorschach and *Körperbau und Charakter* (Physique and character) by Ernst Kretschmer.

As had to be the case with this kind of subject matter, Jung had approached his great theme through prior studies. We may mention, for example, his 1913 lecture at the Munich Congress "On the Question of Psychological Types," which appears in the appendix to volume 6 of his *Collected Works.* This may give some idea of the stages of development that Jung had to go through in this effort. And this comment tells us something further about the process:

"What I say in this book has been tested, so to speak, sentence for sentence in the practical treatment of patients and also came out of that to begin with. ... Therefore the layman should not be blamed if certain conclusions seem bizarre to him or even if he goes so far as to believe that my typology is the product of an idyllic, undisturbed study chamber."[42]

What is it that distinguishes Jung's typology from that of the others? He looked for his answers to the question in the relationship of a person under study to his environment and other people. Thus he asked if an individual was directed more toward or more away from the world around him, if he was to be considered *extraverted* or *introverted.* At first glance, this approach seems almost simplistic, though it cannot be denied that this question already engages essential basic attitudes that distinguish the character of one individual from that of another. The introvert is sometimes characterized by a hesitant, self-directed, withdrawn quality, a tendency to take the defensive rather than the offensive, to observe rather than act. The overall point is that the introvert is – as the word already tells us – oriented inward. The attitude of an extravert, by contrast, is marked by a pronounced outgoing, seemingly open, and accommodating quality. An extravert is easily at home in any situation, is quick to form relationships, and frequently ventures in a carefree and trustful manner into unknown situations, heedless of any misgivings.

Rapid decision making seems to rank ahead of careful consideration. We can conclude from this that in the case of the introvert it is the subject, and in the case of the extravert, the object, that assumes primary importance in the life of the person so characterized.

The voluminous tome *Psychological Types,* parts of which Jung revised over the years, develops these two typological descriptions, introducing them by means of intellectual and historical examples. Here already the distinction between the introverted and extraverted character type emerges as a key to understanding historical personalities. We may well count Jung himself an introvert, considering that the real events of his life story, which was so rich also in terms of outer destiny, took place on the stage of inner experience. In this connection, a remark on the nature of his literary opus is illuminating: "All my writings may be considered tasks imposed from within; their source was a fateful compulsion. What I wrote were things that assailed me from within myself. I permitted the spirit that moved me to speak out."[43]

Now obviously it is by no means adequate – in the last analysis, no typology is adequate! – only to inquire into the attitudinal type of a particular individual. As his research went on, Jung hit upon further distinct qualities that could be added to the attitudinal type (extraverted or introverted) so as to constitute a more complete picture of a personality. This further step involves asking which of four *basic functions* is the predominant one. According to Jung, there are two rational functions, thinking and feeling, and two irrational functions, sensation and intuition. At first glance, one might think that only eight different permutations are possible – for example, an introverted thinking type and an extraverted thinking type, and so on for the three remaining functions. Through a process of careful investigation and practical testing, however, further variations may be discriminated: for example, a dominant function and a supportive function.

In addition, the author of the typology recognized the need for a more precise definition of the fluid concepts employed by analytical psychology. This task was to be fulfilled by the definitions included in the book's appendix. There Jung states that an experimental methodology "never has and never will" succeed in capturing the essence of the human psyche. Thus, a true picture, which does justice to the changeability and complexity of the psyche, also cannot be achieved by even the most ingenious typology. Still, the material in *Psychological Types,* which Jung jokingly remarked was "as hard to understand as it is thick," served him in his practical work as a "critical apparatus."

Correct. am Titelblatt.

Prof. Dr. C. G. Jung

Küsnacht-Zürich
Seestrasse 228

Psych. Typen

Gegenstand dieses Buches ist hauptsächlich das Bewusstsein, dessen Orientierungsfunctionen und dessen typische Einstellungen. Das hauptsächliche Gegensatzpaar der Extraversion und Introversion wird dargestellt anhand von Beispielen aus der antiken und mittelalterlichen Geistesgeschichte, der Litteraturgeschichte, der Aesthetik und Dichtkunst, der Philosophie, der Menschenkenntniss, der Biographik und der Psychiatrie. Ein umfangreiches Kapitel ist der Beschreibung der verschiedenen psychologischen Menschentypen gewidmet. Zur Erleichterung des Verständnisses ist dem Ganzen eine alphabetisch geordnete Sammlung von Definitionen der hauptsächlichsten Begriffe beigegeben. Das Unbewusste ist jeweils an jenen Stellen berücksichtigt, wo dessen compensierende Function erwähnt werden musste. Der Zweck des Buches ist die Aufklärung der Ursachen für die Vorurtheile und die verschiedenen psychologischen Voraussetzungen, welche das Verstehen des Andersdenkenden und die Verständigung der Menschen unter sich behindern.

Handwritten draft for the introduction to Jung's Psychological Types *(1921). The author was guided in his several years of typological study by the thought: "Denying the existence of types in no way countervails the fact that they are actually there."*

The Psychologist Goes Traveling

"We always require an external standpoint in order to make effective use of the lever of critical mind. How could we, for example, become aware of our national peculiarities if we never once had the occasion to see our nation from the outside. To see it from the outside means to see it from the point of view of another nation. I only begin to understand Europe, our greatest problem, when I see how I as a European do not fit in with the rest of the world. I have my acquaintance with many Americans and my journeys to and in America to thank for an unending amount of insight and critical penetration into the nature of Europe. It is as though there is nothing more useful for a European than to look at Europe from the top of a skyscraper."

This comment by the author of *Psychological Types* might seem bewildering at first blush, especially if we consider that Jung in no way ever gives us cause to doubt his classification as an introvert.

However, we might well be pressing introversion into far too narrow a pigeonhole if we take as the only valid understanding of it what Lao Tzu describes, in a markedly introverted vein, in the forty-seventh section of his renowned *Tao Te Ching* (in the English of D. C. Lau):

Without stirring abroad
One can know the whole world;
Without looking out of the window
One can see the way of heaven.
The further one goes
The less one knows.
Therefore the sage knows without
having to stir,
Identifies without having to see,
Accomplishes without having to act.

In any case, the investigator of the problems of the psyche and its underlying ground did not spurn the chance to undertake a series of extended voyages, deliberately planning for some of them. Quite rightly, Jung's collaborator Aniela Jaffé, whom we also have to thank for recording Jung's memoirs, comments: "Like every real introvert, Jung enjoyed the positive sides of extraversion – travel and success – and even on a large scale." When, for example, he traveled with Freud to America to lecture at Clark University, he wrote to his wife from there (September 1909): "We are the men of the day here. It does one a lot of good to be able to live out this side of things for once. ... My libido is enjoying it in a big way."

Soon after the end of the First World War, when he was still occupied with writing *Psychological Types,* he traveled for a few weeks in 1919 to England. Among the few letters of a purely private nature that have been published is one to his daughter Marianne, who had just turned nine. Her communicative father described to her very vividly how people lived in London and what special features the city where the king and queen lived had to offer. The following year, Jung was invited by his friend Hermann Sigg, a Swiss businessman, on an excursion to North Africa. The route led to Tunisia via Algiers. While Sigg attended to his business, Jung traveled on his own into the interior of the country, southwards toward the Sahara. Finally he had arrived where he always had longed to be, "in a non-European country where no European language was spoken and no Christian conceptions prevailed, where a different race lived and a different historical tradition and philosophy had set its stamp upon the face of the crowd. I had often wished to be able for once to see the European from the outside, his image reflected back to him by an altogether foreign milieu."[44]

An entirely new world opened up before him, even though the distance from cities under civilized influence was hardly greater than twenty kilometers. The psychologist, who had been accustomed to riding since the time of his military service, climbed on a mule and was soon outside the narrow strip in which French was spoken. One thing Jung contrived to do was spend time sitting in an Arab café away from the main streets, observing the people, their speech, their expressions, their gestures. He experienced it as a great loss that he was unable to understand the

"My time in Italy was magnificent and fruitful from several points of view. I found a number of very pretty things in the Museo Civico in Verona," Jung wrote in a letter to Freud on October 20, 1910. On the way home by bicycle, he spent the night at Arona on the south shore of Lake Maggiore. A significant dream that he had there caused him to return home (now by train) immediately, so as to be able to continue his work on Transformations and Symbols.

View of Sousse Harbor (1920): "In March [1920], we traveled to Algiers. Following the coast, we reached Tunis and from there went to Sousse. . . . I was now finally where I had often yearned to be."

Below: Market in Kairouan, Tunisia, about 1920. In a letter to his wife, Emma, Jung described 'a coming and going of red, white, yellow, blue, brown mantles, white turbans, red fezzes . . . faces ranging from white and light yellow to deep black."

indigenous language. Nonetheless, this short trip to North Africa was an important first experience with a foreign psychological reality. Among other things, what strongly moved him was the alteration of the sense of time and the immediacy, rich in feeling, that he felt he perceived in the people of North Africa. Some of these impressions were recorded in *Memories, Dreams, Reflections:*

"The deeper we penetrated into the Sahara, the more time slowed down for me; it even threatened to move backward. ... My encounter with Arab culture had struck me with overwhelming force. The emotional nature of these unreflective people who are so much closer to life than we are exerts a strong suggestive influence upon those historical layers in ourselves which we have just overcome and left behind, or which we think we have overcome."[45]

For him, it was like being immersed not only in an alien sphere of life, but also in a layer of the Middle European psychic past. For the psychologist seeking to attain clarity concerning the nature of the collective unconscious, this was an important experience. Therefore, after the return via Algiers and Marseilles, Jung resolved to take advantage of future opportunities to investigate terrain untrodden by Western civilization. This he was to do in New Mexico, in East Africa, and – in different life circumstances – in India. There is much to suggest that Jung's travels were a kind of modulated continuation of the crisis-filled "nocturnal sea journey" of the soul that he had narrowly made it through.

Extended travels represented a scheduling problem for the physician and psychotherapist. His clientele had grown, and a long interruption in therapy could not be imposed on every patient, even though colleagues might fill the gap for short periods. Nonetheless, his longing to come in contact in their own setting with people living close to nature and the earth was great. Four years later, in 1924, it became possible to take another excursion. This time it was to North America, to the Pueblo Indians of New Mexico. American friends who were financing the project accompanied Jung to the Taos pueblo. Among the dwellings of these "city-building" Indians, who live in large adobe structures, the impressions of nature were powerful, the atmosphere mysterious. This time, real dialogue was possible, for Ochwiay Biano (Mountain Lake) himself spoke English. He introduced Jung to the solar religion of his people:

"We are a people who live on the roof of the world; we are the sons of Father Sun, and with our religion we daily help our father to go across the sky. We do this not only for ourselves, but for the whole world. If we were to cease practicing our religion, in ten years the sun would no longer rise. Then it would be night forever."

From this point of view, this sense of

A café in Tunis. Though he did not speak the native language, this visit was a welcome observation point for the depth psychologist to study the language of gestures.

"My next journey led me, in the company of some American friends, to the Indians of New Mexico." Indians dancing in San Ildefonso, New Mexico.

Middle: Indians in Taos, New Mexico (about 1925).

Below: Indian pueblo in Taos, New Mexico.

responsibility for man, earth, and cosmos, the Indian's devastatating critique of the mentality and decadent morality of the white man became understandable. It is as though scales fell from the eyes of the son of the Reformed Church parson as he realized how the Conquistadors and colonialists and those who had followed on the heels of the Christian missions to the heathen had exploited and enslaved the Indians. He comments:

"If for a moment we put away all European rationalism and transport ourselves into the clear mountain air of that solitary plateau, which drops off on one side into the broad continental prairies and on the other into the Pacific Ocean; if we also set aside our intimate knowledge of the world and exchange it for a horizon that seems immeasurable, and an ignorance of what lies beyond it, we will begin to achieve an inner comprehension of the Pueblo Indian's point of view. ... That man feels capable of formulating valid replies to the overpowering influence of God, and that he can render back something which is essential even to God, induces pride, for it raises the human individual to the dignity of a metaphysical factor. "God and us"..."[46]

The eighty-two-year-old Jung gave us a glimpse of the powerful effect his meeting with Ochwiay Biano must have had on him, when, thinking about the spiritual needs of modern man, he wrote, "We are in urgent need of a truth or a self-understanding like that of the ancient Egyptians or like that which I found still alive among the Taos Pueblo Indians."[47]

The knowledge gained by Jung on these first voyages was immediately applied in his daily psychotherapeutic work. It also came into his efforts as a writer and lecturer. His lecture "Mind and Earth," which he gave in 1927 to the Society for Free Philosophy, part of Count Hermann Keyserling's circle in Darmstadt, as well as his Zurich talk "Archaic Man" (1930), express some of these new insights, as does his lecture in Prague in 1928, "The Spiritual Problem of Modern Man" should be mentioned here. Jung once remarked in this connection that man moves

ANTONIO MIRABAL
TAOS PUEBLO
TAOS, NEW MEXICO

Oct. 7-1932

My dear friend Dr. Jung
Many moons gone by since
I ear from you. I been thinking
of you many times to write to you
but I lost your address and I didn't
had any way of getting your address
until Mrs. Schevill came to see me
last week she is from Berkeley Calif.
The first thing I done was to ask
her your address, and got it. I learn
she was in Switzerland and see you. I
accomplished many important matter
for my peoples since I see you.
You know I was in poor health
when I meet you, but now I am
intirelly well again. I can fight

"For the first time in my life, it seemed to me, someone had drawn me a picture of the really great man ..." Jung is referring to Ochwiay Biano (Mountain Lake), in the photograph below in traditional costume. He corresponded with Jung under his legal name, Antonio Mirabal.

At the Acropolis.

away from his original animal roots to the extent that he advances toward a higher consciousness.

There is another observation that Jung made in America. He felt it could be safely assumed that white Americans had been strongly influenced psychically partly by the Indians and partly by the blacks.

"Thus the Americans present us with a strange picture: a European with the style of a black and the soul of an Indian. He shares the destiny of all usurpers of foreign soil. Certain Australian aborigines claim that it is impossible to take possession of foreign territory, because in the foreign territory live foreign ancestral spirits, and these ancestral spirits will incarnate in new-born children. There is a great psychological truth in this. The foreign country assimilates the conqueror. ... It is the nature of virgin soil everywhere that, if nothing more, the unconscious of the conquerors sinks to the level of the autochthonous inhabitants. Thus in Americans there is a gap between conscious and unconscious that is not to be met with in Europeans, a tension between conscious advanced culture and an unconscious primitivity."[48]

During a stay in England, where he was presenting a seminar, Jung made the decision to make a trip to tropical Africa as soon as possible. To this end, he acquired the traveling documents necessary for Kenya and Uganda from the English Mandatory Administration. Two younger colleagues, an American and an Englishman were prepared to accompany him. Jung realized that this East African journey was to be a major undertaking and one not lacking in danger. In such cases he was in the habit of consulting the I Ching, the ancient Chinese wisdom text and oracle, which had shortly before (1923) been translated into German for the first time by Richard Wilhelm. Using small reeds in place of the traditional yarrow stalks, Jung drew the fifty-third hexagram. Al-

In the company of some foreign friends, in the autumn of 1925, Jung undertook his journey to Kenya and Uganda.

Left: With the Englishwoman Ruth Bailey (middle), a nurse who would later care for Jung in his old age, and the American safari-hunter George Beckwith.

Right: With Helton Godwin Baynes, one of his traveling companions, on the sea crossing.

Some of the time, he was accompanied by forty-eight native bearers and a military escort composed of three men – for example, when he undertook a trek of several days to the foot of 4300-meter-high Mount Elgon.

though this hexagram signals some kind of menace ("The wild goose gradually approaches the plateau. The man sets forth and does not come back."), Jung decided to take up the challenge. And as we learn from his detailed account, the oracle text was to prove accurate.

On 12 November 1925, the party reached Mombasa on the east coast of Africa. Jung went ashore with his companions and pushed ahead along adventurous routes into the region of Mount Elgon, into regions that no white man had yet entered. He had extraordinary experiences of nature. He felt a sense of enchantment. It seemed to him he had returned to the long-lost land of his youth, but with a strange emotional sense that the black man here in remote Africa had been awaiting the meeting with him for five thousand years. In contrast with the short journey to North Africa, Jung had prepared himself this time at least to the extent of learning some Swahili so that he would be able to converse with the natives of the Elgon region. And in fact, he did succeed in making contact with this strange people, in observing their lifestyle

Jung with natives in the border region between Kenya and Uganda, late 1925.

Further impressions from East Africa: "A thousand thoughts buzzed in my head . . . This forced me to let all my observations and experiences pass before me again in review, so that I could note their inner relationships."

Middle: Nairobi, Sixth Avenue about 1930.

Below: "My traveling companions and I were granted the good fortune of experiencing the primeval world of Africa with its extraordinary beauty and its just as profound suffering before it was too late."

and their veneration of the sun and moon. He was moved by the overwhelmingly powerful sense of the divine he encountered there, an experience inconceivably remote from the piety of a European.

At one point he found himself in the midst of an uneasy situation involving warriors excitedly wielding swords, spears, and clubs. He let himself be drawn into the excitement until he again became fully aware of his identity, thus evading the danger of "going native," losing his ego in the archaic collective psyche of the black man. Jung realized once again that

there are limits to one's ability to enter into a strange mentality and that the return journey, in both senses, from the country of the psychic past to the clear-cut precincts of human rationality must be undertaken. He had such an experience of ordered structure in a mosque as he was returning home via Cairo.

Here again were immediate experiences that would have to be integrated and made his own over several years before the empirically oriented psychologist would feel justified in presenting the results of his investigations to the public.

Above: Old Cairo with a view of a mosque (about 1925). "Thus the journey out of the African interior into Egypt became for me like a drama of the birth of light that was very intimately bound up with myself, with my psychology. This was an enlightenment for me, but I did not feel capable of grasping it in words."

Above left and below: Jung in Egypt (1926).

Lieber Otto!
Besten Dank für die treff-
lichen Pläne! Du wirst wohl
bereits von Max meine neuen
Pläne vernommen haben. Ich
bedauere, dass Du den Plan
schon fix und fertig gezeichnet
hast. Ich hatte nur gemeint, eine
provisorische Bleistiftskizze zur
Orientierung für den Zimmer-
mann. Sein Voranschlag be-
trägt nur einmal für's Allgemeine allein 12 M. Das
ist bei Weitem zuviel. Ich muss
aber mich ganz auf den Gedanken eines blossen Refugiums
beschränken. Ich wäre Dir
dankbar, wenn Du meine Skizze
genau nach Vorlage in grösserm
Maasstab zuhanden des Zimmer-
manns zeichnen würdest. Könn-

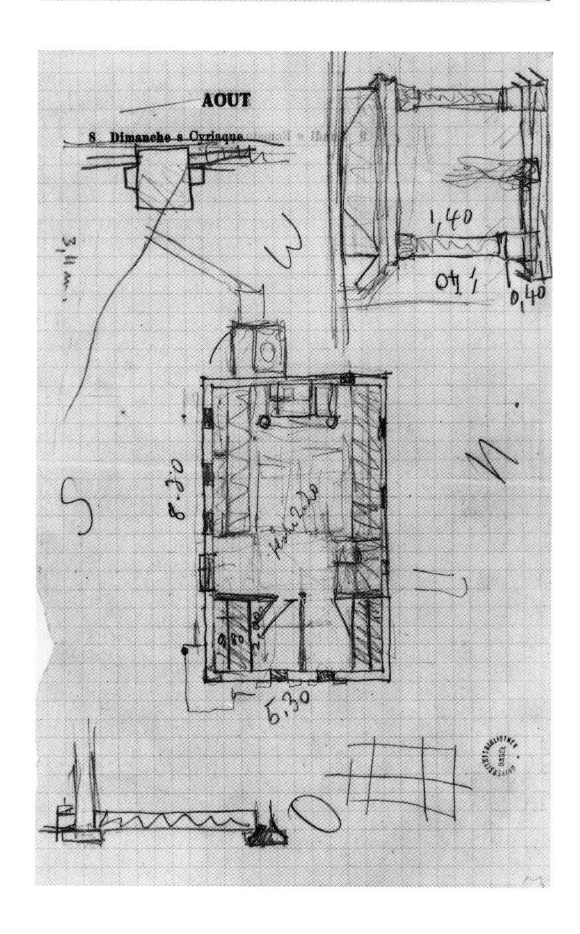

This undated sketch by Jung shows that there was also a conventional variant of his plan for the refuge at Bollingen.

Above right: In this postcard of December 27, 1920, Jung makes it clear to his friend Otto Duthaler that he intends to limit himself "entirely to just the idea of a refuge," presumably also for financial reasons.

Below right: Jung's sketches for a floor plan that was never actualized.

TOWER-BUILDING ON LAKE ZURICH

Vocatus atque non vocatus
deus aderit

In June of 1909, C. G. Jung moved with his family into the house in Küsnacht that had been built by his cousin Ernst Fiechter, an architect. At that time he had the above motto chiseled into a stone over the front door. The formulation comes from a response of the oracle at Delphi and is found in a collection of Latin aphorisms and proverbs by ancient authors. In English it means, "Invoked or not invoked, the god is present." When he was only nineteen years old Jung acquired a volume of such texts published by Erasmus of Rotterdam. This particular saying was to accompany him from then on. It was intended especially to make clear that whoever crossed that threshold would meet not only "No. 1," the personality of Carl Gustav Jung the doctor and psychotherapist, the scholar and, as he once jocularly referred to himself, the middle-class good citizen who just happened to be living at Seestrasse 228. Whoever entered this upper-class, sumptuously appointed house would also encounter "No. 2," the in many ways enigmatic person whose roots reached into hidden depths. For this reason, with many people Jung was a bit strange, not least as a result of his intuitive way of sensing

The tower at Bollingen after the first phase (left) and the second phase (right) of construction. "In Bollingen I am at home in a way that corresponds to my inmost nature."

things and his extensive knowledge ranging into occult and esoteric domains.

The needs that arose in him from the hidden side of his nature required special outlets and also the building of a secluded refuge. It could be said that this was a place he needed for his ongoing self-development. At the beginning of the 1920s he began looking around for a suitable spot. It had to be not too far away from his home and yet lie out of range of the curious observers or insistent visitors who were always plaguing the now-famous man. It was also clear to him that he had to build the new house with his own hands, for the building he had in mind would have nothing in common with a vacation house. The construction of the house was for Jung an expression of his self-development.

It was not long before he found the appropriate spot. That it would have to be next to the lake was clear from the outset. The seemingly enchanted island in upper Lake Zurich to which he had so often sailed in his boat, where aquatic life of all kinds – wild ducks, plovers, and crested grebes – had found a home in the reeds, at first seemed to present the ideal location. But then a piece of land in Bollingen, also on upper Lake Zurich, came up for sale. Jung seized the opportunity and acquired the property in 1922. His building plan ripened gradually. Originally he had thought of a kind of hut, such as are common in primitive societies, "a dwelling place that corresponds to the primal human feelings. It should provide a sense of protectedness, not only in a physical sense but also psychologically."

The construction site proved to be ideal, open to the lake but on the landward side screened off from the village by trees and bushes. There was no need for an architect this time, since the owner and eventual inhabitant would have to follow his own intuition on the path of individuation, and this would have to begin in the construction itself. Nonetheless, some helpers were indispensable. Two local workers assisted him with the heavy labor and mason's work. Dr. Jung learned to split stones at the nearby Bollingen quarries. Anyone who saw the tall man in his late forties, dressed in gray work clothes and working with hammer and trowel, would have taken him for a rural construction worker. Particularly, no one would have thought that the stone and construction work as such could have anything to do with psychology. And yet, in a

very personal way, this was exactly the case. Not a hut, but a tower with a round outline began to take shape. Jung confesses in his memoirs:

"From the beginning I felt the Tower as a place of maturation – a maternal womb or a maternal figure in which I could become what I was, what I am and will be. It gave me a feeling as if I were being reborn in stone. It is thus a concretization of the individuation process. ... It might also be said that I built it in a kind of dream. Only afterward did I see how all the parts fitted together and that a meaningful form had resulted: a symbol of psychic wholeness.

September 1st 1952.

Mr.Don L.Stacy,
453 West 19 Street,
New York City 11. N.Y.

Dear Mr.Stacy,

If granite were at hand I would use it, but in the place where I live we have a hard, bluish-green sandstone which for my purpose is just solid enough.

I'm no artist. I only try to get things into stone of which I think it is important that they appear in hard matter and stay on for a reasonably long time. Or I try to give form to something that seems to be in the stone and makes me restless. It is nothing for show, its only to make these troublesome things steady and durable. There is not much of form in it, chiefly inscriptions and yo would learn nothing from it.

Sincerely yours,

Above: The cube-shaped stone at Bollingen.

Below left: In his letter to Don L. Stacy, Jung stresses that he does not see himself as an artist (cf. p. 72).

Above right: Jung working as a mason.

Below right: A relief on the tower.

It had developed as though an old seed had sprouted and grown."[49]

Here the meaning and purpose of this project is clearly expressed. The reference to the mother principle – here of course to be understood as an aspect of the mind – like the explanation of the circular shape as an expression of wholeness, speak for themselves. Here also a family consideration must be added: two months before the beginning of construction, Jung's mother, Emilie Jung-Preiswerk, died. In her last years, she had kept her own household in Küsnacht. She had been especially close to her grandchildren and, as a former parson's wife, had actively contributed to their religious training.

Jung repeatedly made clear that nobody could spare him the bother of the construction work with its considerable physical demands. In his memoirs, he gives detailed accounts of this work. It is of course very helpful if, in addition to the descriptions in the memoirs, one can get a personal impression of the tower on the spot. One sees that the building is a com-

plex made up of several parts, which took shape in a succession of different phases and projects. These were undertaken at four-year intervals – beginning in the year of his mother's death and ending after the death of his wife Emma Jung in 1955 – until the building reached its present form. Thus there is some sort of mysterious connection between the tower and the deaths of the two women.

From all this, it is clear that the tower at Bollingen cannot be judged according to the usual criteria, either architecturally and aesthetically or in terms of function. For the person who sought refuge here again and again was in fact not the Professor Jung known to everyone. It was No. 2, the personality that seemed to be rooted in "the beyond," in some remote past of the soul. Thus in his memoirs Jung remarks:

"At Bollingen I am in the midst of my true life, I am most deeply myself. Here I am, as it were, the "age-old son of the mother." That is how alchemy puts it, very wisely, for the "old man," the "ancient," whom I had already experienced as a child, is personality No. 2, who has always been and always will be. He exists outside time and is the son of the maternal unconscious. In my fantasies he took the form of Philemon, and he comes to life again at Bollingen."[50]

Alive also, at least for the owner of the house, were its protective spirits. The ancient Romans called them *lares* and *penates*. Also in this connection, one has to have looked around in person and seen the open hearth in the smoke-blackened kitchen, which must have smelled of porridge and smoked bacon, of all kinds of spices, and occasionally also of wine. For here Jung lived fully, and differently also from how people live today in modern, plastic, built-in kitchens. In such a place of course there is no room for household spirits and the like. As Jung put it, "Lares and penates are important psychological quantities, which if at all possible should not be frightened away by too much modernity." Thus he had no need of electricity. He could make do with an open fire and lanterns. And what need was there for running water? Water could be drawn from the well. Anyway, who wanted to be distracted from his woodcutting and firemaking, his water-pumping and cooking, by people who brought the annoying speed and jumpiness of the rationalized technical world with them into this place of refuge and self-discovery?

Thus it was not only on his journeys to the Native Americans and Africans that the psychologist was strongly drawn to nearness with the elements and nature and

C. G. Jung in his Bollingen home. From right to left: carving stone; tending the fire; splitting his own firewood.

to contact with simple things. This was the world that Jung had to remain emotionally in contact with, at least at special times. In his Bollingen tower, this was ensured. This need of his for contact with the primal level of things was understood by only a few people. One of them was the Africa expert Laurens van der Post, who often spent time with the doctor from Küsnacht. He was familiar from his own experience with Jung's relationship to things and with the particular way he had, for example, of relating to fire. In his book on Jung, he writes:

"He never took it for granted. It always remained a miracle for him and was sacred for him. He had a way all his own of layering the wood and kindling the fire. There was something in it of the way primitives, with much difficulty, made fire, preparing it with endless patience, as if it were a matter of life and death and once lit must not go out. Jung did this instinctively, as though he were performing a religious rite. Then when the Hindu flame flared up, his face in its light bore an expression of piety like that of some prehistoric priest."[51]

To the adventure of building the tower and living in it was added Jung's sometime occupation as a stonemason. Impressive evidence of this are stone monuments and inscriptions engraved in stone, which can be seen on the tower itself or in its immediate vicinity. Closer inspection of the figures and texts that are found on the stones shows that they, too, are connected with his real work, with the process of maturation that had to be undergone. Altogether, it is difficult not to see both the inside and the outside of the tower at Bollingen as a kind of shrine of the modern mysteries. Jung never saw himself as an artist. In a letter of 1952 he wrote: "I am only trying to cut things in stone that . . . seem to me important to preserve in a solid material, so that they can last for some time. Or I try to give form to that which seems to be alive in the stone and makes me restless. It is nothing for display purposes; it is only there to provide these disquieting things with solidity and duration."[52]

The tower at Bollingen in its present form.

Right: The image of Philemon, drawn by Jung. "In my fantasies [the "old man"] took the form of Philemon, and he comes back to life again at Bollingen."

The tower at Bollingen – various views.

The interior: "Lares and penates are important psychological quantities, which if at all possible should not be frightened away by too much modernity."

Above: Alchemical illustrations of the transformation process: The king and his son with winged Mercury in the middle.

Right: The symbolic figure of Hermes in the form of a magician, here as the guardian of the fire that brings the sun-related masculine principle and the moon-related feminine principle into union.

THE ENCOUNTER WITH ALCHEMY

In his effort to place on firm ground his personal experiences – including often breathtaking dreams, fantasies, and visions – Jung had long been on the lookout for historical prefigurations. He was concerned, among other things, with the question, "Where are my ideas to be found in history?" As already recounted, he found support initially in early Christian gnosticism. Gnosticism was important to him because it had a notion of God and man that seriously considered the polarity of light and dark and masculine and feminine. Jung, occupied with gnosticism particularly between 1918 and 1926, came more and more to have the impression that the living flow of tradition between ancient Gnosticism and the present time had remained unbroken. Rather than having dried up, it had become an underground spiritual current for which a new bed had to be forged.[53] Jung's reopening of the study of alchemy may be considered a success in just this regard.

Alchemy is a traditional way of knowledge, the rich symbology of which in many ways corresponds to the data of depth psychology. Alchemy is concerned with the great theme of transmutation, with the preparation of the "philosopher's stone" *(lapis philosophorum).* We should not, however, make the mistake of associating it with some misguided method of producing gold. Like spiritual astrology, it is part of the great body of Western esotericism that has the mythical figure Hermes Trismegistos, "thrice-great Hermes," as its spiritual figurehead. As the poet Alexander von Bernus, a contemporary proponent of alchemy, characterizes it:

"The background of alchemy is initiation, a training in the mysteries that reaches back over millenia. In pre-Christian times, it was part of the psychic store of the Egyptian-Chaldean-Hellenic shared world consciousness; later it flowed into the West via Arabic culture and became tinged with the content of Christianity. ... Certainly transmutation is the focal point of the alchemistic path of initiation; but this does not refer to the transformation of metals. Rather it is the inner, mystical transmutation process of which the external chemical-physical transformation of metals is only the manifestion, become visible and real within the material sphere."[54]

Jung's interest was directed neither toward this early phase in the history of chemistry and metallurgy nor toward the spiritual exercise that lay behind it and that the alchemist had in mind when he

made use of chemical images and processes. Here, too, Jung was trying to fulfill his task as a psychotherapist. As "an eminent historically oriented researcher" (Aniela Jaffé), he was looking for an objective basis for what he personally had learned from his experiences. His inner experiences could not be left suspended in some vacant middle air. The gnostic tradition had, on account of the problematic nature of its source material, proved inadequate as an objective basis. At this point, at the end of the 1920s, the sinologist Richard Wilhelm came to Jung and brought an ancient Chinese Taoist treatise to his attention. The English title is *The Secret of the Golden Flower,* an esoteric text that was still hardly known at that time. Wilhelm felt sure that the German translation he had made of the text covered only a part of what had to be presented. Consequently, he expressed the wish for Jung to provide an interpretation of the text. The two scholars had met in Darmstadt on the occasion of a meeting of Count Keyserling's "School of Wisdom." Jung had already been interested in Taoist esotericism, especially in the form of the ancient Chinese wisdom and oracle text, the *I Ching,* which Wilhelm had also translated into German and which Jung made use of quite a few times, especially at decisive moments of his life.

Thus Jung was not unprepared when Wilhelm sent him *The Secret of the Golden Flower.* This event was also preceded by a significant dream, which caused him to paint a mandala of a "golden, well-fortified castle," an expression of a goal and its fulfillment. Jung was deeply moved by the arrival of the manuscript: "I immediately devoured the manuscript, for the text brought me an unanticipated confirmation of my ideas about mandalas and the encircling of the middle. That was the first event to break through my aloneness. Here I felt a kinship, something I could connect with."

Not only did this lead to a collaboration between the two men that lasted until Wilhelm's premature death, but also the Taoist text seemed to have an effect that worked on Jung like an initiation. Only after this experience was he able to engage intensively with the alchemical tradition. This should be emphasized here, because the psychoanalyst Herbert Silberer, in his book *Probleme der Mystik und ihrer Symbolik* (Vienna 1914, translated as *Hidden Symbolism of Alchemy and the Occult*

An illustration from the Amphitheatrum Sapientiae Aeternae *of the German alchemist (and Rosicrucian) Heinrich Khunrat (1560 – 1605), which brings together the two operations necessary for alchemical activity: the* oratorium *(i. e., the fundamental meditative approach) and the* laboratorium *(on the right), the site of practical work.*

Below: Abraham Eleasar as one of the many fictitious alchemists, in hieratic trappings.

Pages 76 – 77: The stages of the alchemical process according to the Aurora Consurgens, *a 15th century text discovered by Jung.*

Arts), had already pointed out the relevance of hermetic, Rosicrucian, and alchemical material. But it was from Wilhelm that Jung received the impetus to illuminate the parallels between alchemy and depth psychology.

Through his Munich book dealer, he was able to acquire extremely rare alchemical works. These were partly collections of texts from the sixteenth and seventeenth centuries. Today they make up a considerable part, numbering more than two hundred volumes, of the private library left by C. G. Jung. Anyone examining Jung's later work finds that it is not only in the two major works *Psychology and Alchemy* and *Mysterium Coniunctionis* that Jung was concerned with alchemy. In his other writings, he continually refers to alchemical ideas and adduces them as comparisons to present-day productions of the unconscious. In order to be able to do this, the psychologist had first to bring to fruition a time-consuming pioneering labor. The alchemical style of expression, its terminology and its imagery, is full of enigmas and totally impenetrable obscurities. Not even every alchemist was able to understand the veiled texts of his colleagues. Jung tells us what difficulties he had to struggle with before alchemy began to be able to fulfill the role in his own work that he hoped for. In his memoirs, we read on this point:

"It was a long while before I found my way about in the labyrinth of alchemical thought processes, for no Ariadne had put a thread into my hand. Reading the sixteenth-century text, *"Rosarium Philosophorum,"* I noticed that certain strange expressions and turns of phrase were frequently repeated. For example, *"solve et coagula," "unum vas," "lapis," "prima materia," "Mercurius,"* etc. I saw that these expressions were used again and again in a particular sense, but I could not make out what that sense was. I therefore decided to start a lexicon of key phrases with cross references. In the course of time I assembled several thousand such key phrases and words, and had volumes filled with excerpts. I worked along philological lines, as if I were trying to solve the riddle of an unknown language. In this way the alchemical mode of expression gradually yielded up its meaning. It was a task that kept me absorbed for more than a decade."[55]

During this period, he made the not inconsiderable effort needed to read through the greater part of the classical literature of Western alchemy, including many volumes in Latin. In this way, important sources for his research into the unconscious and its processes became available. It became clear to the psychologist that these ancient texts, in which the alchemists spoke of different kinds of matter and material transmutations, were "a grand projective depiction of unconscious thought processes," representations of inner perceptions. The experiences of the alchemists could almost be identified with his own experiences, albeit in a different context and expressed in different terms. An astounding parallelism began to emerge. What his work with gnosticism had not been able to accomplish was now vouchsafed to him in the form of alchemical ideas. This was the missing link in spiritual and intellectual history that he had been looking for.

Jung was cautious enough not to present his (re-)discovery to the public immediately. Several years passed, and even then he proposed his first results only tentatively for discussion – for example, at the Eranos conferences in Asconia-Moscia on Lake Maggiore in the years 1935 and 1936, that is, to a relatively small inner circle of psychologists and representatives of the humanities and sciences. The lecture "Individual Dream Symbolism in Relation to Alchemy" (1935) is an attempt to bridge an intellectual gap. Dream images of a contemporary person are presented and then amplified through images from alchemy. In his lecture of the following year, "Religious Ideas in Alchemy," Jung pointed to a significant correspondence between the philosopher's stone sought for in alchemy and Christ, that is, the archetype of the Self. But it required a further, often difficult, process of clarification over several more years before Jung was able to produce the manuscript

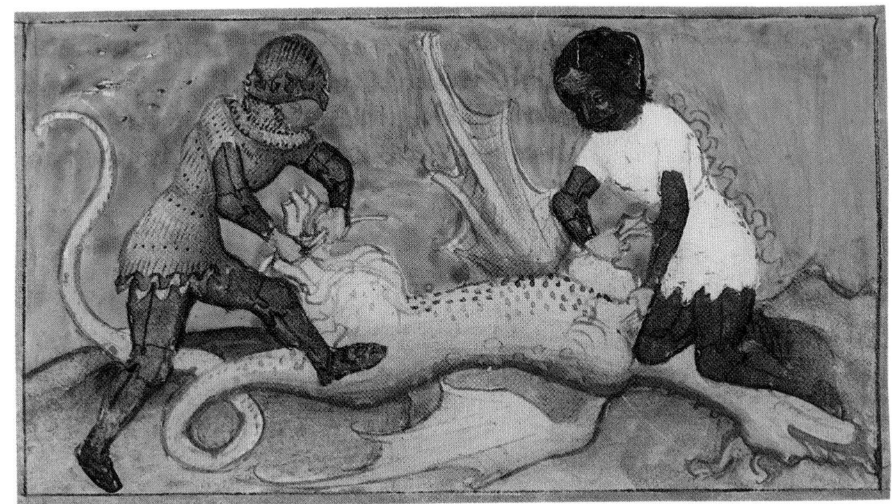

of *Psychology and Alchemy,* which he placed in the printer's hands in 1944.

This marked the fruition of a long process of research and observation of himself and others. Jung's collaborator, the classical philologist Marie-Louise von Franz, who came to Bollingen when she was still a young student, assisted Jung in the translation of many Latin and Greek authors. They also studied the pictorial material with which the ancient authors had attempted to illustrate what could not be expressed in words. Jung occasionally remarked that the astounding parallels between the productions of the unconscious of contemporary man and the conclusions of the alchemistic seekers is already visible in the correspondences of form and content that exist between dream images and particular alchemistic engravings.

The longer Jung persisted in his special studies, the more convinced he became that alchemy – at least the Western, Christianity-tinged variety – is an esoteric undercurrent of orthodox Christianity. In other words, this kind of alchemy is related to the more familiar Christianity of the Church as dreams are

Top: This group photo, of uncertain date, might be from the 1930 meeting of Count Keyserling's "School of Wisdom" in Darmstadt, Germany. C. G. Jung is second from the right.

Left: Marie-Louise von Franz, who edited and commented on Aurora Consurgens *(Zurich 1957).*

Right: Title page of Rosarium Philosophorum *(1550).*

ROSARIVM
PHILOSOPHORVM.
SECVNDA PARS ALCHIMIÆ
DE LAPIDE PHILOSOPHICO VERO MODO
præparando, continens exactam eius scientiæ progreßionem. Cum Figuris rei perfectionem ostendentibus.

AEGIDIVS de VADIS . Dialogus inter Naturam et Filium Phil.
Theatr. Chem. 1602 II p. 122 . Sequentia post p. 30.

LAVRENTII VENTVRAE VENETI . De ratione conficiendi Lapidis Philosophici, Liber. Theatr. Chem. Vol. II. 1602. p. 244

Once Jung had recognized the significance of alchemy for his researches, he not only collected old texts, but took many notes from alchemical writings. The notes shown here are from the second volume of the famous Theatrum Chemicum *(1602), which is mentioned in* Psychology and Alchemy.

related to consciousness. And just as the dream compensates, in a symbolic fashion, for the conflicts of everyday conscious life, so alchemy strives to bring to the surface something of the tension of opposites that is present – whether acknowledged or not – in Christianity.

Such a problematic situation is evident, for example, in the case of the trinitarian image of god that has come down to us. It has been pointed out, not only in feministic theological circles, that the feminine principle is missing from this image. Or again, Christianity treats the factor of darkness or evil as though it lay outside the will of God. Consequently, the devil appears as a dark splintering-off, as the shadow of a God of light. In this regard, Jung reflects: "Evil needs to be taken into account just as much as good, for after all, good and evil are nothing but idealized extensions and abstractions of action, both of which belong to the light-and-dark phenomenon of life. Ultimately, there is no good out of which no evil can come and no evil out of which no good can come."[56]

This is not the first point at which it becomes obvious that Jung, haunted from his earliest youth by numinous fantasies and dreams, had no choice as a psychologist but to make the religious dimension part of his realm of research. Moreover, he had to relate to it in the forms in which it repeatedly manifests in the human psyche.

Another factor that is part of every therapeutic event that touches the depths of the unconscious and that is also found in alchemy is *transference.* In volume 16 of *The Collected Works of C. G. Jung,* which appeared in 1958 and for which the author was still able to write a foreword, this theme, so important for the practice of psychotherapy, is presented with the help of a series of alchemical images. Simply speaking, in transference the patient "transfers" onto the analyst feelings and sensations formerly associated with a person who played a role in his childhood, such as his father or mother.

The problems related to transference had already occupied a place of importance in the psychoanalytic theory of Sigmund Freud. For Jung also, transference is a "mode of relationship" that always requires an actual partner and does not at all arise in relation to the figures, authorities, and processes of purely inner psychological experience. From this point of view, the process of individuation that stands at the center of analytical psychology cannot be brought to completion without a state of relatedness of the individuating person to another human being or to society.

"The unrelated person has no wholeness, for this is reached only through the psyche, which in turn cannot exist without its other side, which is always in the partner, the "thou" *[du].* Wholeness arises out of the combination of I and thou, which appear as aspects of a transcendent unity, the nature of which can only be comprehended symbolically – for example, through the symbols of the circle, the rose, the wheel, or the *coniunctio solis et*

The "invisible college" of the Rosicrucians, from Speculum Sophicum Rhodo-Stauroticum *(1618) by Theophilus Schweighardt.*

Below: The title page from Salomon Trissmosin's La Toyson d'Or *(Paris 1613). It contains important alchemical symbols.*

Opposite: The cosmic man (puruṣa), seventeenth-century Nepalese painting on fabric.

lunae [the union of sun and moon in alchemy]."

By "relatedness" Jung clearly does not mean an identification or synthesis of two individuals, but rather "the conscious connection of the I with everything that is present as a projection in the partner, or 'thou'. This means that the development of wholeness is indeed an intrapsychical process, but one that is *essentially* dependent on the relatedness of the individual to another human being."[57]

In this connection, we might think of Martin Buber's philosophy of dialogue, which speaks of the "sphere of betweenness," the fullness of being face to face that arises again and again in meeting: "Becoming I, I say thou. . . . In the thou, a person becomes I." (M. Buber)

It goes without saying that in this process the archetypal relationship of man and woman, the masculine and feminine, or in Jungian terminology, the animus and anima, plays a primary role. Becoming whole, realizing the Self, brings the meeting between animus and anima to the level of the *mysterium coniunctionis* (mystery of union), called in mysticism the "mystical marriage," and in alchemy, the "chemical marriage."[58]

In the last analysis, such a name also applies to every profound human encounter – as rare as it is that this (karmic) quality of eternity arises into consciousness. Religions speak of these things, the folk mysteries speak of them, and analytical psychology speaks of them, too. It may have been in this regard that Jung wrote in his letter of 12 August, 1960: "The living mystery of life is always hidden between two, and this is the true mystery that words cannot tell and arguments cannot exhaust."

Jung's Relationship With Eastern Spirituality

Much older than the problems between East and West in the sphere of politics is the tension between the European mentality and Asian spirituality. In considering this problem, the religious and spiritual traditions of the Far East deserve particular attention. This is by no means a specialized problem for academics; it is a question that concerns all humankind, from both Eastern and Western Hemispheres. These two branches of humanity are on the way toward each other. On their encounter and their dialogue, which can be regarded as a process of panhuman self-knowledge, many important things depend. It often appears that this totality of mankind is leaving the duties of both present and future to be fulfilled exclusively through economic, technological, and organizational measures. But this way changes the world only from the outside. There is, however, a process of transformation involving individuals and entire nations of people that is not less important and that must take place "inside." The two processes are inseparable.

It is in this connection that Jung's relationship to Eastern spirituality acquires meaning for the present. It has long been pointed out, accurately enough, that the Swiss psychologist contributed greatly toward intensifying Western interest in Eastern spirituality. There is no doubt that such a claim has more to it than the fact that Jung's solution of the riddle of alchemical dream symbology was inspired by the sinological labors of Richard Wilhelm. The need to engage the spiritual traditions of the East imposed itself on Jung from another side – in connection with the ever-recurrent theme of wholeness or individuation. The Asians' differently disposed structures of consciousness, reaching back into the psychic past, seemed to Jung suitable for shedding light on particular psychic manifestations of Western man. Though it exhibits definite extraverted tendencies, introversion has

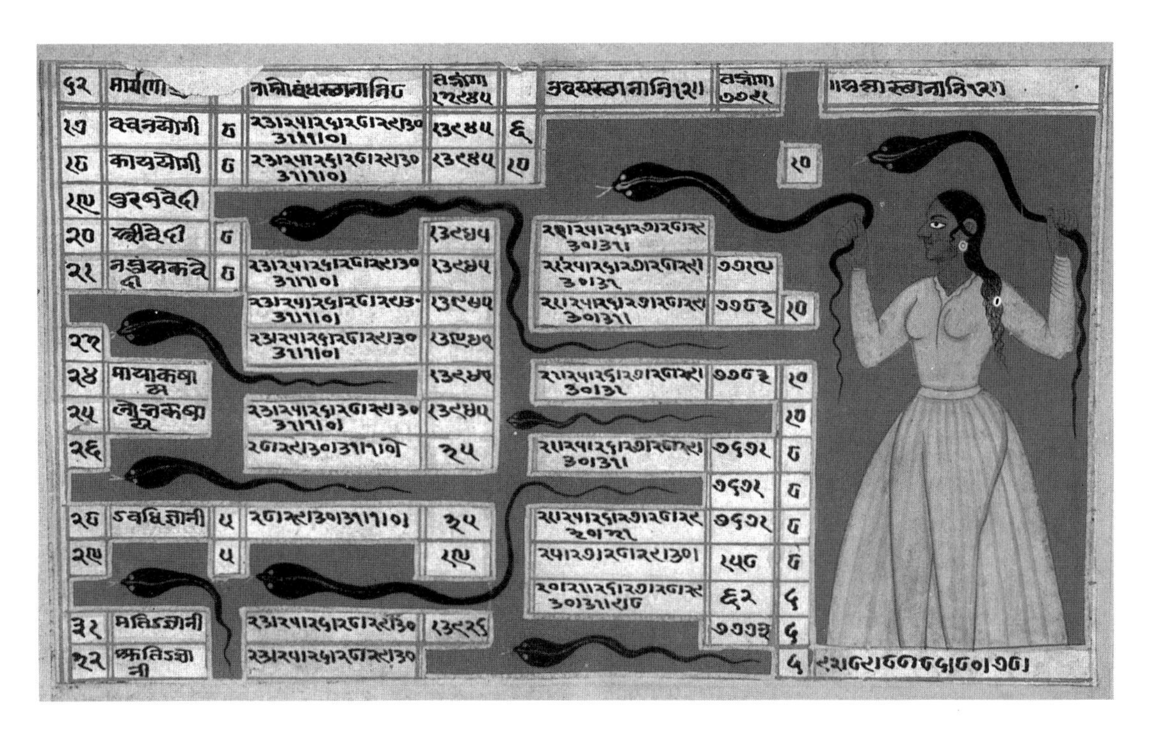

Goddess holding serpents in her hands. Eighteenth-century Indian tantric art.

Opposite: The goddess Ganga with chakras. Seventeenth-century Indian tantric art.

for centuries been the dominant psychological posture of Eastern man. Jung, however, could hardly be classed as a superficial champion of the Eastern approach, even though some religious historians and ecumenicists (W. Visser 't Hooft, and E. Benz, for example) have labeled him as such. And there have been others who have wanted to place him in the all-too-numerous throng of yoga freaks and Zen snobs. Jung's real intentions and his goals as a medical psychotherapist hardly admit of such suspicions.

C. G. Jung did, in numerous works of his, take positions on various questions concerning the psychology of Eastern and Western religion. In the weighty eleventh volume of his *Collected Works,* appropriately titled *Psychology and Religion: West and East,* he devotes himself to this subject. But before we look into Jung's observations on general and specific problems of Eastern spirituality, we must ask what significance he himself attributed to his work in this area. Clarification here is especially desirable, because the misrepresentation of Jung's supposedly syncretist tendencies mentioned above may well derive from misunderstandings on this point.

In his foreword to the second edition of his psychological commentary on Richard Wilhelm's translation of the Chinese treatise *The Secret of the Golden Flower,* Jung takes the opportunity to point out the kind of misinterpretations that even educated readers of this classic book had fallen into:

"It has happened a number of times that people have thought that the purpose of publishing this book was to put in the hands of the public a method of attaining beatitude. Such people have then attempted – completely ignoring everything I said in my commentary – to mimic the "method" of the Chinese text. Let us hope that such representatives of this spiritual low point were but few."[59]

Jung saw a second misunderstanding in the opinion that in his interpretation he had simply explained his own special psychotherapeutic method, "which according to this view consist in suggesting Eastern ideas to my patients as a means of effecting their cure. I do not think that my commentary provides any pretext for this kind of superstition. In any case, such an opinion is entirely erroneous and based on the widespread view that psychology is an invention with a particular purpose and

"The fact that the East so lightly sets the ego aside seems to point to a mind that cannot be identified with our 'mind.' It is certain that the ego does not play the same role in the East as it does with us."

A procession with sacred relics in Kandy. "Considering all of this, the Eastern form of 'sublimation' goes beyond withdrawing the psychological center of gravity from the ego-consciousness."

not an empirical science." This emphasis on the empirical basis that he claims for his analytical psychology is to be found in many other passages of his works. There is no dearth of documentation for it.

Jung also sought in other contexts to confute these misunderstandings. Typical of his attitude toward the East is, for example, the speech he gave at the commemorative gathering for Richard Wilhelm in Munich on 10 May 1930.[60] In it he calls for understanding for the spiritual culture of the East, for overcoming existing prejudices, and for openness toward the alien spirituality. He called for "understanding devotion, beyond all Christian resentment, beyond all European pretension" in supposing that rationality should be elevated above the East's spiritual, intuitive approach to knowledge. Jung knew from abundant experience that "all average minds" lose themselves either in blindly giving up their own roots or in equally uncomprehendingly attributing blame.

"Spiritual Europe will not be helped by a mere sensation, a new thrill. Rather we have to learn to earn in order to possess. What the East has to give us can only be of help in a labor that is still before us. What good is the wisdom of the Upanishads, what good are the insights of Chinese yoga, if we forsake our own foundations as though they were mistakes we had outlived and rapaciously settle on a foreign coast like homeless pirates?"[61]

Jung is not any less straightforward when, in the same passage, after pointing to the need for a broadening of the Western concept of science, he writes: "We need a real three-dimensional life if we expect to experience the wisdom of China as a living thing. What we need at present is European wisdom concerning ourselves. Our way begins with the European reality and not with yoga exercises intended to blind us to our own reality."

Jung already senses, as early as 1930, that "the spirit of the East is really *ante portas* [at the door]." And he already sees two possibilities in the coming encounter between East and West. There might be a healing power hidden in it, but also "a dangerous infection." Very few people at this time were capable, as he was, of commenting on the ambivalence connected with the East-West question. Five years later, in February 1936, he published in the Calcutta journal *Prabuddha Bharata,* his English-language essay "Yoga and the West."[62] If his collaborative studies with Richard Wilhelm had earlier spurred him on to penenetrate to the essence of the ancient Chinese tradition, this little treatise shows what value he now placed on the psychophysical training system of India. He first focuses his attention on the development that led Western man into the centuries-old conflict between belief and knowledge, between religious revelation and conceptual understanding. Jung observes a "pathlessness that borders on anarchy. . . . European man in the course of his historical development became so distant from his roots that his mind finally split between belief and knowledge, just as every psychological excess resolves itself into pairs of opposites."

This view did not cause Jung to fail to recognize that there are also advantages implicit in this pattern of development of consciousness, advantages that Jung's distinguished student, Erich Neumann, examined more closely.[63] From another viewpoint, Rudolf Steiner[64] before this and Jean Gebser[65] afterward presented the cultural history of mankind as a single great process of transformation of human consciousness. In this context, Jung's researches take on an importance that should not be underestimated.

The conclusions that Jung published in the Indian journal were really aimed at European and American readers: "The split in the Western mind makes an adequate realization of the intentions of yoga impossible from the very outset. The Indian not only knows his nature but also to what extent he *is* that nature. By contrast, the European has a science of nature and knows astonishingly little concerning his own nature, the nature within him."[66] Here again we hear Jung's call for a view of humanity that includes the spiritual dimension and aims toward wholeness. For the rest, Jung focuses on the distinctive psychic dispositions, that of the Asian being entirely different, even though the reservation must be expressed that such general judgments about types are not without problems. Jung's advice was to study yoga carefully as an index of Indian spirituality; but as much care should be reserved for the question of whether and to what extent spirituality that has arisen on Asian soil can be practiced in the West. His thoughts culminate here in an almost prophetic, provocative comment, which should be understood quite literally: "The West will produce its own yoga in the course of the centuries and, indeed, on the foundation created by Christianity." We are left with the question of whether and to what extent this is already taking place. In any case, this statement should be considered when it comes to making sure

West gate of the stupa at Sanchi.

Left: Perahera procession in Sri Lanka (photograph taken about 1938). "Neither in Europe can I make any borrowings from the East, but must shape my life out of myself – out of what my inner being tells me, or what nature brings me."

Impressions from a trip through India.

If I had not been urged by friends living in India I never should have dared to say something about India. My trip was a hurried one, ~~though~~ it was my first visit to India. A first impression of a country is very often the same as when one meets a person for the first time: ~~your~~ the impression may be quite inaccurate, even definitely ~~in~~ wrong in many respects, yet ~~you~~ are likely to perceive certain virtues or certain shadows, which very probably would be blurred by the ~~in~~ more accurate ~~obs~~ impressions of a second or third visit. My reader ~~should~~ would make a ~~big~~ great mistake if he were to take my statements for gospel truth. Think of a man, who for the first time in his life comes to Europe, spends some 6–7 weeks travelling from Lisbon to Moscow and from Norway to Sicily, who does not understand one single European language, but English and who has a most superficial knowledge of the peoples, their history and their actual life. Would he be likely to produce anything more than a wildly delirious phantasmagoria of hasty impressions, snapshot sentiments and impatient opinions? ~~Anything beyond the Ahs and Ohs of the traveller tired by night journeys, choked with dust and harassed by indigestion?~~ I am afraid he would have little chance to escape the curse of utter incompetency and inadequacy. I am very much in the same position with reference to India. I am told that I have the excuse ~~to be~~ of being a psychologist, supposed to see something more or at least something peculiar, which other fellows might overlook. I don't know. I must leave the ultimate verdict to my reader.

A page from Jung's handwritten account of impressions from his journey to India.

"India made a dreamlike impact on me, for I was and remained in search of myself, in search of my own truth. Thus the journey was in effect an intermission in my then intensive occupation with alchemical philosophy."

we are not taken in by hasty solutions. We may think in this connection of such pragmatically intended offerings as "yoga for Christians" or "yoga for the West." Jung obviously had in mind more than some kind of concoction of one part Christianity and one part yoga or Zen. What should such a "yoga" be like, then, that corresponds properly to the consciousness of Western man, that takes sufficiently into account that this is a consciousness that has borne within it for two thousand years the cultural impulse of the Christ event?

Jung did not attempt to provide an answer to this. He did not see himself as the founder of a Western path of initiation. As a doctor, he limited himself to diagnosing this spiritual deficit. It is true that his psychology and psychotherapy embraces the widest possible range of elements and phenomena. But he did not feel the vocation of a cultural innovator or a spiritual guru, even though he has long been viewed as such in certain circles.

It is impossible to ignore certain criticisms of his judgment of the spiritual paths known in his time. We do have commentaries from him on texts from the domain of Eastern religion. He expressed his views in "The Psychology of Eastern Meditation" and wrote a series of detailed forewords to the *I Ching* and to books by, for example, D. T. Suzuki and Heinrich Zimmer. But the religious teachings of the West are, with the exception of late medieval alchemy, often thrown together in an undiscriminating fashion. He mentions in a single breath the "mass imports of exotic religious systems" – the Baha'i faith, the Sufi sects, the Ramakrishna mission, Western Buddhism, Christian Science, the Anglo-Indian theosophy of Helena Petrovna Blavatsky and Annie Besant, as well as the anthroposophy of Rudolf Steiner, which consciously attempted to connect Middle European tradition and contemporary consciousness. This indiscriminate lumping together is regrettable.

Another problem is that no adequate assessment has been made of Jung's analytical philosophy from the point of view of spirituality. There is a need for re-

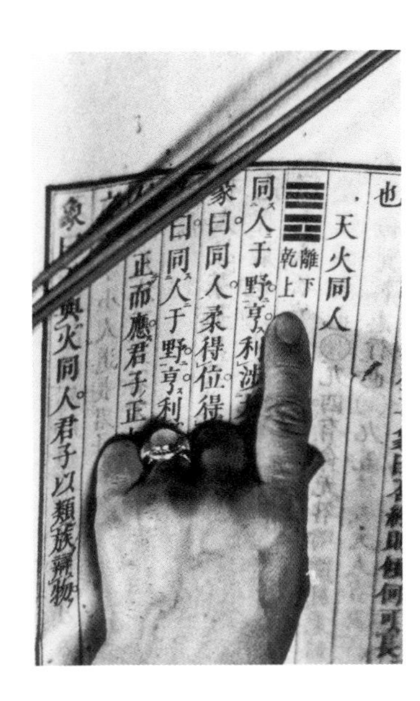

I Ching *divination with yarrow stalks.*

Portraits opposite, from the top:

Erich Neumann (1905 – 1960), depth psychologist (1953).

Heinrich Zimmer (1890 – 1943), pioneer in Indian studies (1933).

Richard Wilhelm (1873 – 1930), Sinologist (1930).

Rudolf Steiner (1861 – 1925), founder of anthroposophy (1911).

ligious thinkers to confront analytical psychology without prejudice and in the spirit of ecumenicism that our current situation so much calls for.

Jung's recounting and interpretation of a dream that he had at the end of his travels in India in 1938 came as a kind of summation of what India and the spirituality of the East meant to him. The dream image in itself had nothing to do with the tradition of the country that he had just come to know personally; rather it is connected with a central theme of Western esotericism – the holy grail. Jung writes:

"Imperiously, the dream wiped away all the intense impressions of India and swept me back to the too-long-neglected concerns of the Occident, which had formerly been expressed in the quest for the Holy Grail as well as in the search for the philosopher's stone. I was taken out of the world of India, and reminded that India was not my task, but only a part of the way – admittedly a significant one – which could carry me closer to my goal. It was as though the dream were asking me, "What are you doing in India? Rather seek for yourself and your fellows the healing vessel, the servator *mundi,* which you urgently need. For your state is perilous; you are all in imminent danger of destroying all that centuries have built up."[67]

The section on India in his memoirs ends with the remark:

"Toward the beginning of spring I set out on my homeward voyage, with such a plethora of impressions that I did not have any desire to leave the ship to see Bombay. Instead, I buried myself in my Latin alchemical texts. But India did not pass me by without a trace; it left tracks which lead from one infinity into another infinity."

This autobiographical note doubtless speaks for itself. In relation to the question with which he had started out on the journey, Jung the psychological researcher and theoretician is making the statement that with all his interest in the Oriental spiritual heritage, he remains dedicated to Western thought.

Confrontation with National Socialism

If one accompanies Jung in his explorations of the mysteries of the human psyche, of the substrata of psychic reality, of the border regions of gnosticism and alchemy, of remote and profound religious experience, one could easily come to the conclusion that he never emerged from the "nocturnal sea journey" of the years after his separation from Freud. One might conclude that, aloof from everyday realities, he led a life of dreams. But this would be to forget his work as a doctor and his vital engagement with the political currents of the 1930s.

In 1933, Jung saw himself as one who "must do the work of a pioneer in a world from which everything original has disappeared." Because of this, engagement with political matters could not play a primary role in the activities of the psychotherapist. But still he did not permit himself to be reduced to "the decent middle-classed Swiss citizen living at Seestrasse 228 in Küsnacht bei Zürich" (as he referred to himself ironically in a letter of 26 May 1934 to his Jewish colleague James Kirsch). As a psychotherapist, he had to take sides during the decisive early period of National Socialism, especially since, from neutral Switzerland, he was able to provide support to the sorely pressed representatives of psychoanalysis in Germany and Austria and thus to depth psychology as a whole. Whether he did this as unequivocally and as clearly as might be wished is questionable as we look back today.[68]

At that time, certain political events took place that spelled the end of the Weimar Republic in Germany: the so-called seizure of power by the National Socialists on 30 January 1933 and the "empowerment" of Adolf Hitler by the Reichstag on 24 March, which for all practical purposes established dictatorship in Germany. With this the fate of psychoanalysis as a "Jewish science" was sealed, even though those involved might have initially thought with Sigmund Freud

Opposite, from the top:

Downtown Bombay, 1941.

C. G. Jung on one of his many excursions in India (1937).

Bombay, Gateway to India (about 1940).

Above: C. G. Jung in an etching by Rabinovitch (1935).

Berlin, February 27, 1933: The burning of the German Reichstag ushered in the National Socialist era.

in 1933 that "maybe it won't come to the worst."

The signs of an increasingly wide base in the population for the "national uprising," as well as its approval by the leadership of the church, are by now well known. The burning of the Reichstag on 27 February 1933 was followed by the establishment of the first concentration camps for the isolation of unwanted elements of the population. On 1 April 1933 came the Nazi-instigated boycott of Jewish businesses. On 10 April, the fires were blazing in heaps of burning books in front of the Berlin Opera and in many other German cities. With the words "against the psychologically destructive overemphasis of the sex life and for the nobility of the human soul," the writings of a certain Sigmund Freud were committed to the flames. Freud's comment that at least he was burning "in the best company" was an expression of profound resignation. Anyone who was familiar at this time with the program of the National Socialist Party, and who had not only read Hitler's *Mein Kampf* but also – as few did – took it seriously, already sensed something of the magnitude of the peril for mankind, especially for the Jewish minority.

Certain remarks by Jung from this period are striking as reflecting more than mere foresight. As one who had attentively followed the political events of the time in Middle Europe, he wrote as early as November 1932, on the eve of the Nazi takeover:

"We are threatened on a horrifying scale by wars and revolutions that are nothing other than psychic epidemics. Millions of people might at any time be overcome by madness, and then we will have either a world war or a devastating revolution. Instead of being prey to wild animals, avalanches of rocks, or flooding waters, man is now prey to the elementary forces of his own psyche. The psyche is a great power that many times exceeds all the powers of the earth."[69]

The psychological diagnostician saw "the blond beast," the "Germanic barbarian," rising up with elemental force. The collective man was threatening to suffocate the individual:

"... the individual on whose responsibility all of the works of mankind finally rest. The mass as such is always anonymous and irresponsible. So-called leaders [*Führer*] are inevitable symptoms of a mass movement. The real leaders of mankind are always those who are aware of themselves and reduce the momentum of the mass at least by their own weight by holding themselves consciously apart from conformity to the blind natural laws of masses in motion."[70]

These sentences are part of a lecture that Jung gave in February 1933 in Cologne and Essen in which he tried to show the relevance of psychology for the

The square in front of the Berlin Opera, May 10, 1933: National Socialists burning so-called "un-German" writings and books. Sigmund Freud: "At least I'm burning in the best of company."

current situation. In retrospect, we cannot say that the voice from Switzerland was understood. The mass movement apostrophized by Jung had already been unleashed. The "conformity to blind natural law" could no longer be neutralized.

Events began to take place that required more from Jung than an analysis based on depth psychology or social psychology. The psychotherapy movement in Germany, which was fragmented into various schools, needed a representative of international repute who was also scientifically qualified to unite the movement into fruitful activity. In March of 1933 Ernst Kretschmer, professor of psychiatry and neurology at the University of Marburg, resigned from the office of president of the General Medical Society for Psychotherapy. Since Jung already held the office of delegate and since the membership had the necessary trust and confidence in him, it seemed appropriate for him to take over the presidency "until further notice," as it was put. On the National Socialist side, there was Dr. Matthias Heinrich Göring, a student of Alfred Adler's and a close relative of the Prussian prime minister and later field marshal of the Reich, who of course considered himself a National Socialist, but at critical times conducted himself in such a way that his politically imperiled colleagues often experienced him as a "protective shield."

What did threaten the society, however, was the so-called *Gleichschaltung* (forced conformity), which meant compulsory orientation toward the Nazi ideology with its racial principles and the principle of obedience to the Führer. In any concrete case, it was not objective argument that decided, but rather the word of the leader of the Reich and his subordinate administrators. In accordance with this, Jewish and other "non-Aryan" doctors and functionaries in accordance with the "Aryan paragraph," were relieved of their responsibilities – if nothing worse. In this situation a person was required who, beyond

being professionally competent and internationally respected, was able to appear neutral.

This situation created an opportunity for Jung. As a Swiss, he took advantage of it to move toward the formation of an international society of psychotherapists. This meant an organization under the auspices of which relatively independent national societies could be constituted, such as separate German, Swiss, Dutch, and Danish chapters. In this way, naturally, the German national group would still be liable to *Gleichschaltung* and political manipulation, but not the others. Moreover, this would create the possibility that persons could be affiliated with the international society who could not be accepted by any of the national groups. This had the special effect of providing access for Jewish colleagues to the same professional organization in spite of the Aryan paragraph and forced conformity to National Socialist principles.

Certain security measures were also built in. In order to prevent numerical predominance of one nation in the supranational society (the most likely threat would come from the forcibly conforming German group), the statutes devised by Jung stipulated that no national group could represent more than 40 percent of the present votes. Beyond this, Jung endeavored to strengthen the international foundations of the society and to win the sympathies of his Swiss compatriots, whose political shortsightedness he complained of, for the proposed project.

In January 1934 Jung expressed himself in optimistic terms to his Zurich colleague and follower Alphonse Maeder. He believed his plan for the society would make it possible to support the then isolated scientific community of Germany. He wrote:

"Thus I find it necessary for the neutrals on the outside to provide an opportunity for international affiliation by founding a general organization. Germany is presently more closed off intellectually than during the First World War; consequently it especially needs to be connected with the rest of the intellectual world."[71]

This letter is not the only indication that Jung was concerned about more than just a pragmatic formal solution that would meet the needs of the moment. The statutes of the International General Medical Society for Psychotherapy were at last ratified at the seventh congress in Bad Nauheim. At that time, Jung also officially became the president of this "supranational" association. In response to misunderstandings that are occasionally still expressed, it must be emphasized that he actually had nothing to do with the forcibly conforming German national group under Dr. Göring. This can be shown from other documents also.

In a circular letter of 1 December 1934, signed by Jung, the essential was communicated to the medical psychotherapists: It has "been resolved that affiliation with a national group is no more than optional, that is, the possibility exists of individual membership within the framework of the "supranational general medical society for psychotherapy." The "supranational society" is politically and confessionally neutral." It would have been contrary to Jung's nature to consent to any ideological, political, or dogmatic limitations.

It should be realized what practical significance these regulations had during the period of the Nazi dictatorship. The practical importance of the emphasis on supranationality is self-evident against the background of Nazi pressure politics. That Jung persistently followed this policy during the troubled 1930s – he did not resign from the presidency of the society until 1939 – can be documented in various ways. For example, it can be shown that he continued to maintain contact with numerous Jewish colleagues in his immediate circle. Thus he did not hesitate in his book *The Reality of the Soul* (1934) to refer to a work of his Jewish colleague Hugo Rosenthal *Der Typengegensatz in der jüdischen Religionsgeschichte* (The opposition of types in Jewish religious history). A year later, in a plea for "understanding among the various psychotherapeutic schools" published in the *Schweizerischen Ärztezeitung* (Swiss medical journal), he singles out as synoptic works a study by his Jewish colleague Gerhard Adler along with works by W. M. Kranefeldt and Nazi party member Gustav Richard Heyer. In the same article, Jung stresses his concern for the "European," that is, supranational, status of psychotherapy. And when Jung in October 1937 greeted those who had come to Copenhagen for the ninth congress for psychotherapy, he stressed how important it was at that time to open up the widest possible horizons for the young science. He says in his welcoming address:

"With regard to this necessity, any overly narrow restriction to any artificial boundaries would be a catastrophe for our science, whether these boundaries be national, political, linguistic, confessional,

C. G. Jung with Dr. Mathias Heinrich Göring (1934).

Opposite: Nazi party rally, 1935 in Nuremberg. "The collective man is threatening to suffocate the individual, the individual on whose responsibility all of the works of mankind finally rest."

Group photograph from the ninth Congress for Psychotherapy in Copenhagen (1937). First row, from right to left: H. G. Baynes, London; M. H. Göring; C. G. Jung; unidentified; H. Kogerer, Vienna; P. Bierre, Stockholm.

or philosophical in nature. . . . The nations of Europe constitute a European family, which like every family has a particular spirit. No matter how far apart political goals may lie, in the last analysis they are based on a pan-European psyche, the aspects and facets of which should not remain unknown to a practical psychology."[72]

This emphasis on the European and international could not have made Jung appear to the National Socialists as a sympathizer, much less a collaborator. In any case Jung's position could not be made to harmonize with the notion of "Aryan superiority." For the supranational society made possible, indeed fostered, what the forcibly conforming German national group prohibited!

In this connection, we may briefly examine certain episodes the interpretation of which has cast a considerable shadow over Jung. We do not mean to claim here that the Swiss depth psychologist was entirely blameless. Two publications in the *Zentralblatt für Psychotherapie* (Central bulletin for psychotherapy), which was edited by Jung, can be regarded as having particularly triggered pejorative opinion.

One of these publications is more formal. In the December 1933 number Dr. Göring, as the head of the German national group, published a kind of manifesto making submission to National Socialist principles by the German psychotherapists compulsory. Publication of such an article was in fact agreed to by Jung, but, as was logical, it was not intended for publication in the *Zentralblatt,* which was aimed at the general membership, but only for the German supplement. Only the members of the German national group could be called upon in this way to swear a "loyalty oath" in the style of those times. As for the area under his authority, Jung saw no reason why Jewish colleagues should be excluded in the future from collaborating on the journal. For example, at the end of December 1933 he delegated the editing of the review section to Viennese doctor Rudolf Allers. At the same time, Jung considered it tactically skillful to give over the editing of the journal as a whole to a conforming National Socialist representative of the profession.

There was a period of weeks during which the progress of the December number of the journal remained somewhat unclear to those involved, Jung included. During this time, the editor in charge, Hamburg physician Walter Cimbal, neglecting to give Jung, the principal editor, timely notification, authorized the publication of the Göring article on his own. In loyal fashion, Jung took a protective stance toward his editor in relation to third parties. He expressed his own pronounced misgivings, however, in a letter that brings his actual views to light. Thus we read in his letter to Walter Cimbal of 2 March 1934:

"As you will recall, I expressed to you my explicit wish that Dr. Göring should sign the *German* number. As a foreigner, I have no business mixing in German domestic politics. Also, in relation to the foreign subscribers, it is a lamentable tactical error to foist off on already critical foreign readers manifestos concerned purely with domestic politics, which in a pinch can be understood as necessities for Germans. ... I must urgently request you to keep the *Zentralblatt,* which is aimed at foreign circulation, nonpolitical in every respect.[73]

Thus Jung's resolve to be nonpolitical, at least in keeping psychotherapy free from ideological constraints, cannot be questioned. But the deed was done. Jung speaks of the flurry of hostility that the *Zentralblatt* unleashed in Zurich. For, on the one hand, the readers, especially those outside Germany, could not have been aware of the actual background of this oversight (or possibly, intentional set-up of Jung?). On top of that, Jung had made himself vulnerable to attack in connection with the content of the Zentralblatt in another way. In his preface to the third number of 1933, he promised that "the differences between the Germanic and the Jewish psychology, which actually exist and are familiar to reasonable people ... (would) no longer be glossed over. ... I would like to state explicitly that no assessment of Semitic psychology as inferior is implied by this, any more than assessment of the Chinese as inferior is indicated when we speak of the unique character of the psychology of the people of the Far East."[74]

As harmless as this remark in itself might be, especially when taken in the larger context of Jung's work, and even in the context of Freud's psychoanalysis, at this particular time and in view of the personal and situational circumstances, it was liable to nurture some ominous misunderstandings. The effect of this preface was compounded by Jung's sensational essay "The State of Psychotherapy Today," published in the *Zentralblatt* in 1934. Here we find the lines in which Jung communicated his experience with the Jewish race, according to which the Jewish unconscious could only conditionally be considered comparable to the Aryan unconscious. He continues:

"Apart from certain creative individuals, the average Jew is already too conscious and developed to still be impregnated with the tensions of an unborn future. The Aryan unconscious has a higher potential than the Jewish one; that is both the advantage and disadvantage of a youthfulness not yet fully separated from barbarism. In my view, it has been a great mistake on the part of medical psychology up to now indiscriminately to apply Jewish categories, which are not even valid for all Jews, to Christian Germans and Slavs. By doing this, it interprets the most precious mystery of Ger-

Gustav Richard Heyer (1933). "Just on account of being a Nazi, as he told me with a grin, he was able to get Jewish colleagues visas to England up until right before the war. He vouched for two 'suspects' – one had already been arrested and was turned loose. During the War, he took care of Jews ..." (Zoë Heyer to the author, July 19, 1985).

Sigmund Freud at his work table in Vienna (about 1937–38). "The name Freud can never be expunged from the intellectual history of the ending nineteenth century and the beginning twentieth."

manic man, the creative, portentous ground of his soul, as an infantile, banal swamp, whereas my warning voice has for decades been suspected of anti-Semitism."[75]

Does Jung reveal himself here as the anti-Semite that Freud already thought he saw in him? Or does this text, which we cannot analyze more closely here, require a far more cautious interpretation? Let us only point out that the racial superiority of the Aryan postulated by the Nazis is not to be confused with the "higher potential" referred to here. This can be concluded without doubt, and not from the context of this article alone, for a member of an ancient people of culture is more mature, more conscious, than a member of a still relatively undeveloped "youthful" people. That is the idea Jung is expressing. But what associations he inevitably aroused!

The reaction was not long delayed. In the *Neuen Zürcher Zeitung* of 27 February 1934, the Swiss psychoanalyst Gustav Bally launched a vehement attack on Jung in which he mercilessly condemned him. In his article entitled "German Racial Psychotherapy," we read:

"The editor of this *gleichgeschalteten* [forcibly conforming] journal, as he himself confesses, is C. G. Jung. ... A Swiss is thus the editor of the official organ of a society, that, according to the statements of its leading member, Dr. M. H. Göring, "requires of all its members active as writers that they thoroughly study Adolf Hitler's fundamental book *Mein Kampf* in all scientific earnest and acknowledge it as their basis."

That this view is based on a double misunderstanding can only be realized when the circumstances we have recounted are known. This article unleashed an avalanche. Jung responded, also in the *Neuen Zürcher Zeitung* on 13 and 14 March and again with an addition on 15 March. He asks his opponent, to whom others had as-

"Yes, I slipped up," Jung admitted when, after the Second World War, he went to see Leo Baeck (1872–1956), a renowned Jewish scholar, in his Zurich hotel in order to attempt a reconciliation. (See Wehr, Jung: A Biography, *p. 304ff.)*

sociated themselves, to reflect whether, in this situation so dangerous for the cause of psychotherapy, as a cautious neutral he should have resigned, or – as actually happened – should have stuck his neck out and exposed himself to misunderstandings.

An extremely awkward, and at the same time tragic, scandal, damaging to Jung's reputation, had now arisen. But it was Jung who, long before National Socialism with its distorted Germanism arose, had pointed to the dangerous potential inherent in "the blond beast," a potential that of course was not entirely tied to membership in the Nazi party. Jung came to regret making the comments when he realized that his assessment of the different psychologies, coming at such a questionable time, could be construed as outright discrimination against Jews and in fact was so construed.[76] Even a few proponents of analytical psychology fell prey to the contagion of this view.

On the other side, that Jung's actions produced helpful results is undisputed. He was neither a follower of the Nazis nor an anti-Semite. Beyond that, he supported many individual Jews through word and deed. This is confirmed by Aniela Jaffé, who was well informed and also one of the persons affected. But Jaffé, the amanuensis of his memoirs and the coeditor of the main edition of his letters, adds the following:

"The fact that Jung made it [his distinction between Jewish and non-Jewish psychologies] public at a time when being Jewish was a mortal threat, and that he placed psychological-racial distinctions on the agenda of the International Society, must be regarded as a grave error. Though the most abysmal consequences of Jew-hating became known only later, even at that time any suggestion about Jews being different was fuel for further fanaticism. Here the silence that was a familiar part of the doctor and that was so often imposed

The Virgin Mary as Protectress, anonymous woodcut of the late fifteenth century. "The religious need longs for wholeness and therefore lays hold of the images of wholeness offered by the unconscious, which, independently of the conscious mind, rise up from the depths of our psychic nature."

"Protestantism has obviously not given sufficient attention to the signs of the times which point to the equality of women. But this equality requires to be metaphysically anchored in the figure of a 'divine' woman, the bride of Christ."

on him should have been the rule of the day."[77]

Jung, who, as his compatriot Conrad Ferdinand Meyer said, was "not an ingenious book," but rather "a human being with his contradictions," did not shrink from speaking his mind. This he did, for example, after Sigmund Freud died on 23 September 1939 in his London exile, at the age of eighty-two. In the *Basler Nachrichten,* he dedicated a detailed obituary to the Viennese master. In it, praise and blame are interwoven and bound together with an acknowledgement, the effect of which, in 1939, is also worth thinking about. Jung writes:

"In the course of personal friendship that bound me to him over many years, I was granted the opportunity to look deeply into the soul of this unique person. He was a man possessed, that is, one to whom a light once opened with an overwhelming force, taking possession of his soul and never letting go. It was the encounter with Charcots ideas that called awake in him the primordial image of a soul in the grip of a daemon, and kindled that passion for knowledge which was to lay open a whole continent to his gaze. He felt he had the key to the murky abysses of the psyche ... He believed in the powers of the intellect; no Faustian shudderings tempted the hybris of his undertakings. From this sentiment there grew up his astonishing knowledge and understanding of any morbid psychic material ... The name Freud can never be expunged from the intellectual history of the ending nineteenth century and the beginning twentieth."

These lines can be applied word for word – *cum grano salis* – to Jung himself. When he wrote them, the horror of the Second World War had begun. This was a manifestation of forces erupting from the unconscious that would shock all mankind. In the mid-1930s Jung had associated these forces with the archetype of Wotan. The majority of the texts related to this theme are brought together in the voluminous tenth volume of his collected works, *Civilization in Transition.*

Psychology and Religion

Looking at Jung's works superficially, one might gain the impression that the Swiss psychotherapist occupied himself far more intensively with general and specific cultural and religious phenomena than with medicine and psychotherapy. And in fact, in his Collected Works, themes of intellectual history and spirituality take up by far the most space. Setting aside the early psychiatric and experimental work, there is hardly an essay or a book that is not related to these themes. Yet, even when he is comparing contemporary religious experience with the Western or Eastern traditions or with myth and the revealed traditions of various peoples and periods of history, Jung is speaking in his medical capacity, whether as a depth psychologist or as a practicing psychotherapist. He had serious reasons for his occupation with these themes. In a talk that he gave at a conference of Alsatian Protestant ministers in Strasbourg in 1932, which has since become well known and often cited, he said:

"Among all my patients beyond midlife, that is, over 35, there is not a single one whose ultimate problem is not connected with his approach to religion. Indeed, in the last analysis everyone becomes ill because they have lost that which living religions have provided to their believers in all times; and no one is really cured whose connection to religion has not been restored – which of course has nothing to do with any particular religion or affiliation with a church.[78]

Since for Jung God is "a primordial experience of man," religion and psychotherapy are always understood in a broad sense. Therapy does not aim at mere restoration of functionality. The need for a cure can ultimately not be separated from a profound need for salvation, from the question of life's meaning and the longing for wholeness. In this sense, Christianity with its symbolism of salvation is, like all religions of mankind, a kind of psychotherapeutic project. It is from this point of view that Jung's remarks about himself

The Annunciation, painting by Bartel Bruyn (1493 – 1553). Jung was deeply interested in the Virgin Mary. "By having ... special [protective] measures applied to her, Mary is elevated to the status of a goddess and consequently loses something of her humanity: she will not conceive her child in sin, like all other mothers, and therefore he also will never be a human being, but a god."

Among Jung's most important conversation and correspondence partners were Catholic and Protestant theologians, predominantly Catholics.

and his work are to be understood. For example, in his letter of March 1943 to Zurich author Arnold Kunzli, we read: "I am of course a doctor, yet more than that: I am concerned with the salvation of mankind, for I am also a doctor of the soul."[79] And he agrees heartily with an English colleague:

"You are completely right. The primary interest of my work is not treating neuroses but approaching the numinous. It is nevertheless the case that access to the numinous is the true therapy, and to the extent that one attains experience of the numinous, one is freed of the curse of illness. The illness itself takes on a numinous quality."[80]

This approach endows psychotherapeutic practice with entirely new perspectives. It is no wonder that, challenged by critics, Jung sometimes had difficulty making his position clear. His was the position of a scientist who confines himself to experienceable, comparable psychological facts and, precisely because of this, shows reverence toward religious reality, not least toward Christianity:

"I am a scientist, not an apologist or a philosopher, and I have neither the ability nor the inclination to be the founder of a religion. ... As a Christian, naturally I stand on the ground of Christian truth, thus it is superfluous to try to convert me. In my presentation I remain, by my own admission, beneath the level of any religious system, for in each case I go only as far as the experienceable psychological facts permit me. I have no ambition to bear witness to, nor to support, any particular belief. I am interested only in the facts."[81]

From this and other personal testimonies, it unmistakably emerges that – in contrast to Freud, who once called himself "a completely godless Jew," and who still in his old age avowed in himself "a definite attitude of repudiation toward religion in any form or state of dilution" – for Jung the relationship between psychology and religion was a definitely positive one. Of course his attitude toward theology, as it was embodied for him, for example, in his father, was an entirely different matter, especially when this "science" was not backed up by religious experience.

Jung defined what he understood by religion in many ways. One example is provided by the Terry Lectures at Yale University in 1937, in which he characterized it and described its parameters. (These were first made available to a wider public in 1940 in the form of the book *Psychology and Religion* and are now found at the beginning of the eleventh volume of his *Collected Works.*) Here religion appears to him as a particular posture of the human mind and – in accordance with the original usage of the word *religio,* defined as a "careful attention to, and observation of, certain dynamic factors that are construed as 'powers': ghosts, demons, gods, laws, ideas, ideals, or whatever else man may have called those factors that he expe-

Campus at Yale University in New Haven. Here Jung gave the Terry Lectures, published under the title Psychology and Religion: *"For understanding religious things, all that is left to us today is the psychological approach. This is why I am making the effort to melt down historically rigidified ideas and recast them in the light of immediate experience."*

rienced in his world as powerful, dangerous, or supportive enough to make careful attention to them develop, or as great, beautiful, or meaningful enough to pray to with devotion and love. ... Since religion is indisputably one of the earliest and most general expressions of the human soul, it is self-evident that any kind of psychology that is concerned with the psychological structures of the human personality cannot circumvent attending at least to the fact that religion is not only a sociological or historical phenomenon, but for a great number of people is also an important personal matter."[82]

As can be seen, Jung bases his orientation here on the work of Rudolf Otto, the former professor of religion at the University of Marburg, who in his epoch-making work *Das Heilige* (The sacred, 1917) presented numinous religious experience as a transpersonal reality that touches and deeply affects man at the core of his existence. From this point of view, it is impossible to approach religion adequately merely by means of textual interpretations or historically determined conventions. That is why Jung, as a person gripped by the numinous in the depths of his being, measured his own experience against the spiritual traditions of mankind. Thus Jung's position is fundamentally completely different from mere external affiliation with a religious sect or a philosophical school. In this respect, Jung is quite close to Tertullian, the North African church father, who spoke of the *anima naturaliter christiana.* The idea here is that the soul is Christian by its very nature, that a natural religious function is inherent in it, even if the conscious ego of a person proclaims an atheistic view.

Three-faced, or "tricephalic", images symbolizing the divine trinity. "The primary objective I was working toward was a thorough presentation of the psychological insights that seemed to me necessary for the understanding of dogma as a symbol in the psychological sense."

Understandably, the Swiss depth psychologist repeatedly had to refute the accusation that his thesis of the "reality of the psyche" served to encourage a one-sided psychologism. His view that psychic factors exist that correspond to divine figures was regarded by the devout as cheapening. It was objected that religious experiences were "not just psychological," and thus also could not be explained purely by psychological methods.

Jung charged his critics with having diligently overlooked his proofs of the psychic origin of religious phenomena. He claimed they had not read books like *Psychology and Religion* attentively enough. He asked them:

"Where do they get such complete information concerning the psyche that they are able to say "just psychological"? That is precisely the way of thinking and speaking of the Westerner, whose psyche is obviously good for nothing. If it had something worthwhile about it, then they would speak of it with awe. But since they do not, the conclusion must be drawn that there is nothing worthwhile about it. But this is not necessarily and not always and everywhere so – only in cases where nothing is put into the psyche and God is kept completely on the outside."[83]

Then the author of *Psychology and Alchemy* adds in parentheses, "A little more Meister Eckhart every now and then wouldn't hurt!" Here he is referring to the inner perception of the mystic, who glimpses the divine spark in the depths of the soul (or psyche) and waits upon the divine birth in the womb of the soul, that breakthrough "from above" that is inaccessible to man's everyday ego.[84]

In the same connection, Jung warns against cheapening the psyche through purely religious projection in terms of rites and dogma. A projection takes place when instead of turning one's attention inward to where cognition takes place, where one is touched and seized by things, one looks entirely to external symbols, rites, relics, etc. for ultimate meaning. The same of course applies to exaggerat-

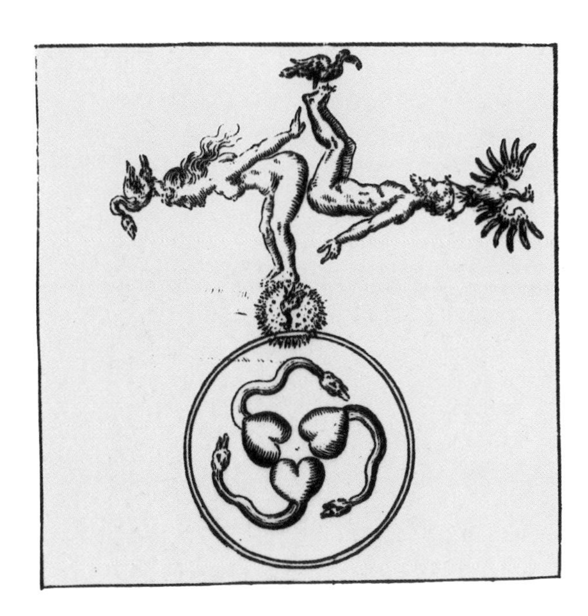

Clavis *(key) from the famous* Musaeum Hermeticum *(Frankfurt 1678) in which triunity is brought together into unity (lower part) with the idea of quaternity, which is based on binarity.*

ing the importance of theological doctrines and creeds, which could result in a rigid religious life fixated on outer forms and formulas. The crucial point is that the psyche must fully participate experientially.

"When the psyche no longer participates directly, religious life rigidifies into forms and formulas. However one conceives of the relation between God and the soul or psyche, one thing is sure: the soul or psyche is not a "just," an "only"; rather it is the dignity a being has, that it is given, of being conscious of a relationship with the divinity. Though it were only the relationship of a drop of water to the sea, even the sea would not exist without the multiplicity of drops."

Clearly Jung's analogous thinking is not entirely without problems. Nevertheless, we can take his argument seriously. It continues: "It would be blasphemous to affirm that God can reveal himself everywhere with the single exception of the human soul. Indeed, the intimacy of the relationship between God and soul precludes any pejorative valuation of the soul from the outset."[85]

In the same passage, Jung himself qualifies overenthusiastic statements he had made in which he perhaps thought he had gone too far in speaking of a relationship of kinship between God and humankind: "but in any case the soul must have in itself a potential for relationship, that is, a correspondence with the divine nature, otherwise a connection could never come about."

Jung then adds the following footnote, directed at his illustrious Swiss contemporary, Protestant theologian Karl Barth: "Therefore, it is psychologically unthinkable that God could be simply 'completely other'; for what is 'completely other' can never be that which is intimately familiar to the soul, which is just what God is. Only paradoxical, or more precisely, antinomic statements about the divine image are psychologically accurate."

In this the depth psychologist is in agreement with the insights of the mystics of all times who have realized the inadequacy of human modes of expression vis-à-vis spiritual experience. Now the question arises, Wherein, as Jung saw it, does the potential for relationship between God and the soul lie? The psychologist's answer is unequivocal – he points to the archetype of the God image. It is the general, human, ordering and meaning-endowing supreme principle, which is capable of infinite development and refinement, a principle that remains unmanifest – it can only be inferred hypothetically; but in symbols, which include concepts of God, this archetype creates ever new forms of expression and appearance:

"The archetype of religious concepts has, like every instinct, its specific energy, which it does not lose even if consciousness ignores it. As we can assume with the highest probability that every person possesses all the average human functions and qualities, so we may also expect the normal religious factors or archetypes to be present, and this expectation does not deceive us, as is readily apparent."

But what is the proper way to approach consciously and voluntarily giving up a tenet or belief? Jung responds, "Whoever succeeds in laying aside the husk of a belief can do it only by dint of the circumstances that somebody else provides him with. ... No one can elude the precedents of human existence."[86]

Jakob Böhme (1575 – 1624), an important post-Reformation mystic and theosophist. Devotional depiction (1677) in an edition of his principal work Mysterium Magnum *(1678).*

Right: Title page of Mysterium Magnum.

An essential reference point is that of (psychic) wholeness. Jung showed to what extent quaternity could be a symbolic expression of this. The archetype of the Self typically manifests itself from time to time according to this quaternary pattern. Jung makes use of the indubitably easily misinterpretable notion of "inner God" to point to the hidden relationship of God and soul. But this term for the archetype of the soul must be regarded as a strictly psychological one, in no way representing any theological or religio-mystical proposition:

"It would be a lamentable error if someone were to construe my observations as a kind of proof of the existence of God. They only prove the presence of an archetypal image of the divinity, and that is all, in my view, that we can affirm psychologically about God. But since it is an archetype of great significance that exercises a strong influence, its relatively frequent appearance seems to be a fact worthy of attention for any natural theology. Since the experience of this archetype has the property of numinosity, frequently even in high degree, it acquires the status of a religious experience."[87]

Here we may draw the reader's attention to an interesting fact. While the central Christian symbol, the embodiment of the divine, is the Trinity, in the unconscious we find quaternity as an embodiment of wholeness. If we now ask who or what the fourth factor represents, we encounter the potency of evil, of the diabolical. Here we touch upon a special problem that must be reserved for dialogue between depth psychology and theology. But this much may be said here: the fourth principle, whether it is the dark principle, the principle of opposition, or the feminine principle that the traditional Christian image of God is lacking (or at least seems to be lacking), it should not be misunderstood as a speculative element in the work of Jung. Even in his late writings (for example, "Answer to Job"), he continued to occupy himself with the theme of quaternity. And the history of religion provided him with additional material. We might mention, for example, the vision of the fifteenth-century Swiss hermit Niklaus von Flüe (Brother Klaus), to whom Jung devoted a short study, or the Silesian Protestant Jakob Böhme (1575–1624), the herald of the fire of divine wrath, but also the messenger of the divine maiden Sophia, that is, the messenger of the feminine aspect of the divine image.[88]

What the psychologist had to say about this subject matter did not flow freely from his pen. On the contrary, what he wrote or communicated in speeches often required long years of testing, meditation, and reflection as well as discussion with colleagues or representatives of other disciplines. Forums for such conversations were provided, for example, by the meetings of the Psychological Club in Zurich or the Eranos conferences, which took place starting in 1933 in Ascona-Moscia on Lake Maggiore and which could not have succeeded without Jung's participation during the first decades. Once the intellectually elaborated material had reached the proper degree of ripeness, it required only the auspicious moment to be formulated and presented to the public.

Above: A view of the lecture hall of the Psychological Club, today on Zurich's Gemeindestrasse.

Below: The Psychological Club was founded in 1916 in this building on the Löwenstrasse in Zurich.

Jung's collaborator of many years Aniela Jaffé tell us of such a situation. It was a radiant August day in the year 1940. The Second World War had been raging for a year. This time the number of those gathered for Eranos was reduced to a small handful. In fact, only a lecture by the Basel mathematician Andreas Speiser had been planned. Hitherto one could count on a dozen or more lectures. But this time, too, it was not to be limited to just one lecture. Jaffé recalls:

"In the afternoon, C. G. Jung, who was among the guests, withdrew to the shady

garden on the shore of the lake. He had fetched himself a bible from the library and was reading and taking notes. On the following day, he surprised the attentively listening audience with a reply to the presentation of his Basel colleague. He complimented it extemporaneously, speaking on the theme "A Psychological Approach to the Dogma of the Trinity." In the manner characteristic of him, thoughtful, sometimes hesitating, he formulated ideas that he had carried around with him for years but had yet to give definitive form. The stenographic record of Jung's improvisations later proved to be nearly ready for the press, except that extensive additions were made. ... Jung's improvisations on the idea of the Trinity concluded the proceedings at Moscia. There followed a conversation, both cheerful and serious, on the terrace of the Casa Eranos with the expansive view of the lake and the mountains. Jung was relaxed and – a rarity, especially in those catastrophic years – content with his performance."

It was the contentment of one who had had his *kairos,* that is, the "hour of fulfillment" necessary for his work and expression. Partly by way of explanation and partly by way of excuse, Jung added the following remark: "I can only formulate the ideas the way they erupt in me. It's like a geyser."[89]

Jung's psychological interpretation of religion, especially of Christianity, is many-faceted. He made a great effort to bring historical symbolic material to bear on his work, but this should not divert our attention from the fact that he sought to work for the present and future by creating awareness. In one of his last works, published for the first time in 1957 in the *Schweizer Monatsheften,* he writes in this connection:

"As at the beginning of the Christian age, now again today we are faced with the problem of a general moral backwardness, in relation to which the modern scientific, technical, and social development has shown itself inadequate. Today too much is at stake and too much obviously depends on the psychological qualities of man. Is he capable of facing the temptation to make use of his power to bring about the end of the world? Does he realize what kind of path he is treading and what conclusions he must draw from the world situation and his own psychic situation? Does he know that he is in peril of losing the life-sustaining myth of the inner man that Christianity has preserved for him? Is it clear to him what awaits him if this catastrophe should come to pass? Is he at all capable of conceiving that it would be a catastrophe? And, finally, does he know that it is *he* who tips the scales? ...

Perhaps a doctor who has occupied himself through his long life with the causes and results of psychological disturbances may be permitted to express his opinion, with all the humility fitting for a single individual, about the questions raised by the *present* world situation. I am neither spurred on by overgreat optimism nor inspired by high ideals; I am just worried about the fate, the weal and woe, of the individual human being, that infinitesimal unit upon which a world depends, that individual being in whom – if we have perceived the meaning of the Christian message correctly – even God seeks his goal."[90]

Many have in the meantime recognized what becomes clear in this passage – that in his last years the Swiss psychiatrist re-

Opposite: Casa Eranos (left) with Casa Gabriela in Ascona-Moscia.

Opposite below: Jung with his wife Emma in Ascona (1933).

Above: At the round table in front of Casa Gabriela (1939).

Below: An improvised talk by Jung on the Casa Eranos terrace (1951).

The atom bomb dropped in Hiroshima on August 6, 1945. "As at the beginning of the Christian age, now again today we are faced with the problem of a general moral backwardness, in relation to which the modern scientific, technical, and social development has shown itself inadequate."

garded the future of humanity with great concern. He had witnessed the unleashing of atomic energy. This happened at a time when most people were talking enthusiastically about the supposedly harmless "peaceful use" of this "clean" energy source. As a psychologist, he ascribed a more devastating potential to the tremendous power of the ideologies and mad ideas of all kinds to which the mass psyche is more or less defenselessly prey.

Considering his awareness of this state of affairs, it is all the more astounding what great hopes Jung had for the future of Christianity. But in view of Jung's approach and his high valuation of the Christ reality, this confidence shows itself as logical and grounded in the psychological nature of this reality. As a psychologist, Jung is thinking of the individuation process, the opportunity for ripening and development that stands before the individual and humanity as a whole. On the other hand, he also has in mind that the central symbol of Christendom, in the Son of God and Man becoming man, took a historical form that also includes a suprahistorical, spiritual dimension. This dimension can become a fact of individual, personal experience at any time, in any place. "In this way, the self-development of man acquires a significance the magnitude of which has still by no means been accurately gauged. But too much external material blocks the way to immediate inner experience," the author of the article adds.

Ironically, it was at a time when theology, especially Protestant theology, was consumed with the problem of the "demythification" of the message of the New Testament, that Jung was pondering the possibilities for further development of the Christian myth – not in the sense of a "remythification" but in the sense of an unfolding of what is set forth in the New Testament itself. For, as Jung says, Western Christianity has "neglected to develop its myth further in the course of the centuries. Those who gave expression to the dark stirrings of growth in mythic ideas were refused a hearing; Gioacchino da Fiore, Meister Eckhart, Jacob Boehme, and many others have remained obscurantists for the majority."[91] Jung's remark is telling us that the esoteric dimension of Christianity requires special attention. It was clear to him that legitimate Christian esotericism cannot at all be replaced as a source of spiritual experience by the outer activities and busy undertakings of the organized churches. Thus Jung advises us:

"A further development of myth might well begin with the outpouring of the Holy Spirit upon the apostles, by which they were made into sons of God, and not only they, but all others who through them and after them received the *filiatio* – sonship of God – and thus partook of the certainty that they were more than autochthonous *animalia* sprung from the earth, that as the twice-born they had their roots in the divinity itself. Their visible, physical life was on this earth; but the invisible inner man had come from and would return to the primordial image of wholeness, to the eternal Father, as the Christian myth of salvation puts it."[92]

How important this insight was for Jung is shown by the Latin inscription on his gravestone, which says that though the first man indeed comes from the earth, the second, the inner man comes "from heaven," that is from a higher dimension of reality. In relation to Jung's life and work, this means that we do him justice only if we consider the efforts of the empirical depth psychologist in conjunction with the personal experiences and insights arising from the roots of his being. It is from here that the transpersonal dimension arises that makes Jung's work so important.

If we wish to pin down Jung's personal outlook more closely as it emerges from the works of the second half of his life, we find it concisely characterized in the words of religious philosopher Raymond Hostie:

"He is a believer but not bound to any particular denomination. He is not bound to any particular denomination, because he rejects the terminology and ritual of the totality of believers that constitutes churches. He is a believer insofar as he remains in search of a coherent body of attitudes and convictions that would express realization of the transcendence of the numinous. Jung's critique of the official, institutionalized religions, which misguide many of their believers as to the meaning and importance of religion, is utterly accurate. His advocacy of discovering a personal meaning, to be reached through an ongoing process, is not less so."[93]

The Jung family grave at the Küsnacht cemetery.

LATER WORK AND FURTHER PERSPECTIVES

Maturation and Later Work

"I do not wish to show anyone else the way, because I know that my way was dictated by something far beyond me. I know that all sounds hellishly grand. ... It *is* grand, and I am only trying to be a humble tool and feel myself to be anything but grand."[94]

This passage from a letter written in 1948 to the English Dominican Victor White sheds light on a man who is in the midst of harvesting the rich fruits of a lifetime of research and converting them to literary output. C. G. Jung was already 73 years old. However, if we look back from that point in time over the long list of books and essays he had published thus far, we find that it represents only a part of Jung's literary opus as it is known to us today. At the end of the Second World War, much of the main body of his work was yet to be published. In short, Jung was clearly one of those creative people whose intellectual productivity does not reach its height until old age.

During the war, when neutral Switzerland was in danger of being taken over by Hitler, as Austria and Czechoslovakia had been, and Jung and his family had sought safety in the interior of the country, a major series of publications came to press. *Psychology and Religion* and "A Psychological Approach to the Dogma of

Opposite: Jung in his study (1946).

An Indian visitor on Jung's seventy-fifth birthday, 1950.

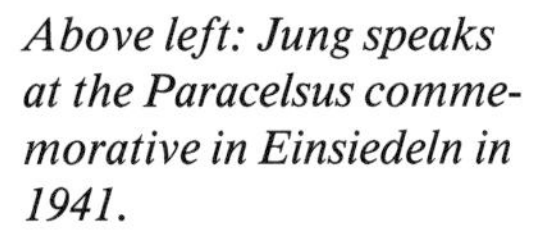

Above left: Jung speaks at the Paracelsus commemorative in Einsiedeln in 1941.

Above right: With mythology scholar Karl Kerényi (1941) in the Eranos garden.

Below: Paracelsus (1493 – 1541).

the Trinity" have already been mentioned. For the anthology *Einführung in das Wesen der Mythologie* (1941, translated as *Essays on a Science of Mythology*) edited with Karl Kerényi, Jung composed pieces showing that the psychology of archetypes is destined to provide a hermeneutic key for the basic experience of the world as manifested in images. The same year, 1941, marked the four hundredth anniversary of the death of Paracelsus (1493 – 1541). For Jung, it meant more than the mere fulfillment of a duty to memorialize his great compatriot and colleague in medical research at the Paracelsus festival in Einsiedeln and Basel. His decades-long occupation with alchemy had also meant a thoroughgoing encounter with Paracelsus. Now he expressed his appreciation of the man from Hohenheim as an intellectual phenomenon the value of which he had recognized as early as 1929:

"He was a powerful gale that tore asunder and swirled together everything that would somehow come loose. Like an erupting volcano, he disturbed and destroyed, but also fertilized and gave life. It is impossible to do justice to him; we can only either under- or overestimate him. That is why we are always dissatisfied with our effort adequately to seize at least a part of his essence."[95]

In these years Jung also made decisions

affecting his teaching work, decisions that were also closely interwoven with his personal life. In 1942, he resigned after seven years from his position as titular professor at the Zurich Confederate Technical College. The University of Basel, at which his grandfather, the elder Carl Gustav, had been active, appointed Jung full professor of psychology, effective 15 October 1943. But in the following year he found himself obliged because of a heart attack to give up this teaching activity as well.

In 1944 *Psychology and Alchemy* appeared, a landmark for research into the subject matter described by the title. For one thing, the book summarized Jung's investigations in this intellectual border region up to that time; for another, it laid the groundwork for further works, such as "Psychology of the Transference" (1946) or *Mysterium Coniunctionis* (1955 to 1956), a late work that was in many ways a summation. In both cases, the author presumed acquaintance with *Psychology and Alchemy,* something that Jung states explicitly in his 1945 foreword. He felt he should once more stress the importance of learning about alchemy's historical "prefigurations," since this could lead to a better understanding of the psyche of contemporary man.

"The reason and inner necessity for this lies in the fact that accurate understanding and evaluation of a problem of contemporary psychology is possible only if we succeed in locating a point outside our time from which we can consider it. This time outside ours can only be a past epoch that was engaged with the same set of problems but under different conditions and in different forms."[96]

Someone examining alchemical literature superficially might come to the conclusion that it diverts attention from present-day problems to a realm that at best might interest a historian with a taste for the remotest possible fringe areas of intellectual history. Jung counters this view with the following argument, written in 1954:

"Research into alchemical symbology, as well as the study of mythology, diverts us from life as little as comparative anatomy diverts us from the life of living men. On the contrary, alchemy serves us as a veritable treasure store of symbols that are extraordinarily helpful for understanding neurotic and psychotic processes. Conversely, through this, the psychology of the unconscious also becomes applicable to those areas of intellectual and spiritual history where symbols are important. It is precisely here that material arises that far surpasses even

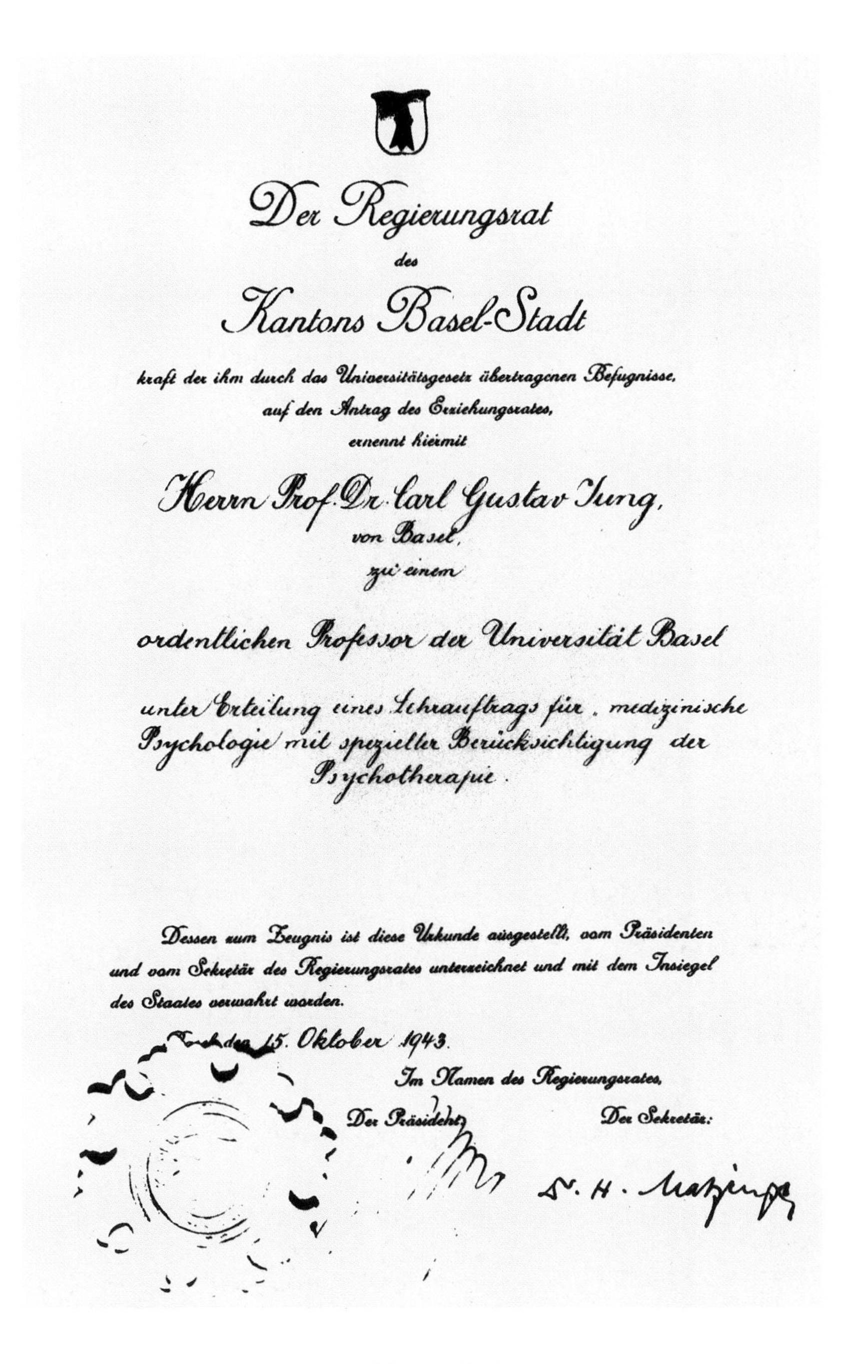

Der Regierungsrat
des
Kantons Basel-Stadt

kraft der ihm durch das Universitätsgesetz übertragenen Befugnisse,
auf den Antrag des Erziehungsrates,
ernennt hiermit

Herrn Prof. Dr. Carl Gustav Jung,
von Basel,
zu einem

ordentlichen Professor der Universität Basel

unter Erteilung eines Lehrauftrags für medizinische Psychologie mit spezieller Berücksichtigung der Psychotherapie.

Dessen zum Zeugnis ist diese Urkunde ausgestellt, vom Präsidenten und vom Sekretär des Regierungsrates unterzeichnet und mit dem Insiegel des Staates verwahrt worden.

den 15. Oktober 1943.

Im Namen des Regierungsrates,

Der Präsident: Der Sekretär:

Dr. H. Matzinger

Jung's official document of appointment to the professorship at the University of Basel.

Mary Churchill, Winston Churchill's daughter, talking to Jung at Allmendingen Castle near Bern. On September 18, 1946, the British prime minister gave his famous speech in the assembly hall of the University of Zurich.

the possibility of therapeutic applications in nearness to life and vital intensity."[97]

Books of Jung's published in the following years include collections of essays that he had already published under the series title *Psychological Treatises.* In these he also included works by such collaborators as Marie-Louise von Franz, Aniela Jaffé, and Riwka Schärf. These were *Symbolik des Geistes* (Symbology of the Mind, 1948), *Gestaltungen des Unbewussten* (Structures of the Unconscious, 1950), *Aion – Untersuchungen zur Symbolgeschichte* (Aion – Investigations in the History of Symbols, 1951).[98] In 1952, the early work *Wandlungen und Symbole der Libido* (Transformations and symbols of the libido, 1912) appeared in a revised and expanded form with its final title *Symbols of Transformation.* This book shows the inner continuity that exists from the early works to the late ones in Jung's basic approach. At the same time, the new fruits of the process of transformation that the author had to undergo are also clearly visible in the book.

This new aspect of Jung's thinking is the result of an inner logic. It is nowhere more clearly to be seen than in the very personal and controversial study "Answer to Job" (1952). Here Jung expresses himself with passionate urgency as a man who opposes the traditional church's idea of God, because, like many others before him (Klaus von Flüe, Jakob Böhme), he has become aware of the conflict of opposites that is hidden in God and that ever and again erupts harshly to the surface. "Answer to Job" is at the same time an answer on the part of the Protestant parson's son who must express his reaction to the Marian dogma that had been promulgated eight years before (1950). Jung acknowledges in an epilogue to this book:

"I was seized by the urgency and major importance of the problem and could not free myself from this. Thus I felt obliged to take up the entire problem, and I did so by describing a personal experience that had been accompanied by subjective emotions. I chose this form intentionally, because I wanted to avoid the impression that I was intending to proclaim an "eternal truth." This book is not meant as anything more than the questioning voice of an individual who hopes or expects to encounter thoughtfulness on the part of his reader."

The response from the theological side, which came out in part in Jung's correspondence during those years, makes it clear that Jung's expectations of thoughtfulness could not (and cannot) be fulfilled by everyone. All in all, the "Answer to Job" represents a challenge to ecclesiastical theology, and it remains to be seen how this challenge will be answered.

Jung, who obviously disregarded possible praise and blame from his critics, at the age of eighty-three had his Zurich publisher, Rascher, print a pamphlet by him on a much-discussed question of the time.

"Flying Saucers: A Modern Myth" referred to the phenomena, observed for decades, known as UFOs (unidentified flying objects). Despite the danger of "putting my laboriously won reputation for truth, trustworthiness, and scientific judgment at risk," he goes on to situate the objects observed in the sky, testified to by many and commented upon from many viewpoints, in a larger spiritual context. He recalls that – according to ancient esoteric tradition – the point of the vernal equinox is moving from the sign of Pisces to that of Aquarius, or, to put it a bit less speculatively, "that the obviously complicated phenomenon [of UFOs] might, along with a possible physical basis, also have a significant psychic component."[99]

In the same year (1958), the publication of Jung's *Gesammelte Werke (Collected Works)* was begun, starting with the sixteenth volume. Thus the elderly man was granted the opportunity of providing his extensive opus, which has since grown to twenty volumes, with a preface. In it, the author recalls once again how closely practical experience and the ascertaining and elucidation of historical material are related:

"In fact, it is a doctor's effort to gain psychological understanding of psychic suffering that, over more than fifty years of psychotherapeutic practice, has led me to all my later realizations and conclusions and that, conversely, has caused me to test and modify my insights in the light of immediate experience. If an unprepared reader were to pick from the series of my later works, for example, an investigation of a historical matter, he would of course have difficulty in discovering its connection to what he conceives of as psychotherapy. Practice and historical reflection are apparently for him incommensurable things. But in the psychological reality, this is not at all the case, for there at each step we encounter phenomena that, when investigated more closely as to their causality, disclose their historical character."[100]

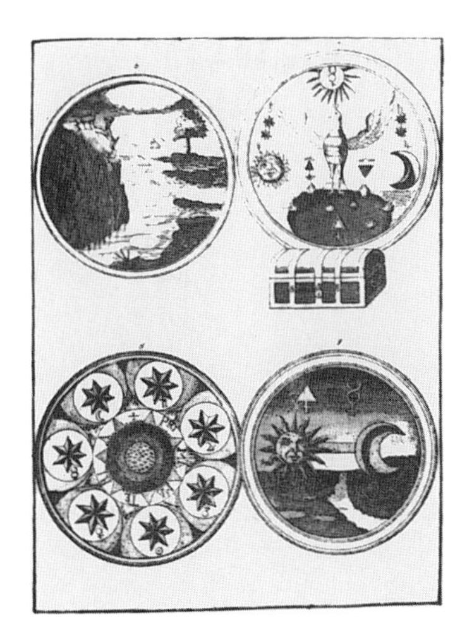

Alchemical symbolic retorts.

Left: Aion, the Hellenistic god of time, to whom Jung dedicated his work of the same name on the history of symbols.

Last Years

After this cursory discussion of what C. G. Jung was able to achieve in his seventies and eighties in terms of literary work alone, it hardly needs to be pointed out that his old age was creative and fulfilled. But even without that, it would not be a highly meaningful remark, because anyone who knew him personally, anyone who saw him in the situations of everyday life, anyone who in any way shared his life, knew that for Jung fulfillment was not a matter of outer activity but of life itself. And he did not equivocate when it came, from time to time, to expressing the actual concrete quality of this life. For example: "My name enjoys an existence that is quasi-independent of me. My real self [however] chops wood in Bollingen and tries to forget about the irritations of an eightieth birthday."

How excellent for him that he had the Bollingen tower as a place of refuge where he could – more than at his home in Küsnacht – be completely himself. For where else could he escape to from the continuous stream of visitors, where else could he go where the postman would not bring a bundle of letters from all over the world every day? But the inward-turned old man still needed contact, in person as well as by letter, despite the fatigue of old age that set ever narrower limits even to this, to say nothing of the illnesses that were leading him toward the boundaries of human existence, but which also held extraordinary experiences in store for him.

Precisely because fame tends to develop its own dynamics, however, it was not only advice seekers, pupils, and friends that showed up day after day at Seestrasse 228 in Küsnacht. Newspaper and radio reporters from Switzerland and elsewhere came around to set up appointments. From time to time a television crew appeared. Once, when the BBC paid a visit, Jung sat on the porch in front of the house with Emma Jung at his side. Again and again, he had conjured up the images of the key moments in his life. This time it

At home in Küsnacht with his secretary Marie-Jeanne Schmid.

Left: At the refuge in Bollingen (about 1950).

Opposite: Jung in a pensive mood at the lake in Bollingen.

Doing the television program "Face to Face" with John Freeman of the BBC.

was the same: the absorption of the young doctor in the world of the unconscious, the encounter with Freud and Adler, and so on – until it came time for various practical questions of the sort that it seemed only the "sage of Küsnacht" could answer. Here and there came incidental comments from the English interviewers, such as that he, the octogenarian, reminded him, at least in appearance, of a typical Swiss farmer. A remark lacking in respect toward the "Herr Professor"? Not at all. Amused, Jung agreed: "Yes, there I think you're not at all far off – I've often been taken for one."

And why not! To know the founder of analytical psychology, the "interpreter of the primal symbolism and the individuation process of mankind," it is not enough just to study his books. It would also not have been enough to work with him in the mysterious atmosphere of his Küsnacht study at analyzing dreams and exploring the psychic history of peoples and religions. No, one would have had to accompany him to Bollingen and be there as he tilled his corn field, as he did stone work, as he felled trees, chopped firewood and piled it up by the front door, as he cooked his food . . .

But Bollingen also was not a treasure store of exquisite wisdom during Jung's lifetime, not even for him, the incorrigible sceptic (or at least truth-seeker), who on the verge of his eightieth year could say of himself:

"I look at myself in the silence of Bollingen and with the life experience of, soon, eight decades, I must confess that I still have not found any neat answer to the question of myself. I am still in doubt about myself and more so the more I try to say something definite. It is as though precisely through that that one is separated even further from knowing oneself!"[101]

Thus he remained the seeker. In the same year as his eightieth birthday, which was arranged with great love and attention but proved exhausting for him, he had the most painful experience of his life. On 27 November 1955 his wife Emma died. She had not only been his life's companion, but also had accompanied him on the often perilous inner path. She was a colleague who drew on her own therapeutic experience; she had published an independent work of her own, an interpretation from the point of view of depth psychology of the legend of the grail.[102]

The widower expressed his great shock at the loss in a letter to his friend Erich Neumann in Tel Aviv: "The shock I experienced is so great that I can neither concentrate nor recover my ability to express myself." Then he tells of a kind of enlightenment, a "great enlightenment" that had stunned him two days before Emma's

Grandfather Jung has not forgotten how to engage in creative play with his grandchildren.

Left: The love of elementary things remains: "The more uncertain I become about myself, the more my feeling of kinship with all things increases."

death and had given him a flashlike glimpse of the mystery of life that was embodied in this woman. Now Jung had no doubt: "I cannot think otherwise than that the enlightenment came from my wife, who at that time was for the most part unconscious, and that the tremendous illumination and sense of release of my insight in turn affected her and was one reason why she was able to die so painlessly and regally. The quick and painless end – only five days between the final diagnosis and death – and this experience have been a great comfort to me. But the stillness and the audible silence about me, the empty air and the infinite distance, are hard to bear."[103]

By the end of 1955 the rich harvest of Jung's life work was almost complete. His major work *Mysterium Coniunctionis,* in which the great themes of the union of opposites and the realization of wholeness resound for the last time, had been concluded. The volume containing the first part had just been published. Jung, however, who had always been so active, could not yet rest. There was still work to do. He had to complete his book about the UFO phenomenon. The edition of his complete works was undertaken, the English, or rather, American version before the German one. While the editorial work connected with this, which required judicious care, was in progress at the publisher's, Jung allowed himself to be convinced to write one more book to accompany the complete works – the autobiography *Memories, Dreams, Reflections.* Basically this was a collaborative project, which he shared with his personal secretary Aniela Jaffé. Starting in the spring of 1957 the weekly sessions began for which an afternoon was always reserved. What came out of this was an

Above: On his eightieth birthday: The procession of well-wishers seems endless.

Right: The inevitable after-dinner speech at the birthday celebration.

esoteric book in the strict sense of the word, because it is not primarily Jung's outer life and times that it documents, but rather what he inwardly perceived and realized as a force that deepened his knowledge and transformed his life. Jaffé makes the following comment:

"The genesis of the book to some extent determined its contents. Conversation or spontaneous narration is inevitably casual, and that tone has carried over to the entire "autobiography." The chapters are rapidly moving beams of light that only fleetingly illuminate the outward events of Jung's life and work. In recompense, they transmit the atmosphere of his intellectual world and the experience of a man to whom the psyche was a profound reality. I often asked Jung for specific data on outward happenings, but I asked in vain. Only the spiritual essence of his life's experience remained in his memory, and this alone seemed to him worth the effort of telling."[104]

Among the significant labors of his last years was one that was for him more intimately interwoven with his essential existence than any book can be. This was the tower at Bollingen. He had had the impulse to build it the year his mother died (1923). At intervals of about four years, he respectedly worked to "complete" the house. Now, after Emma's death and after a time, when nothing had been changed on the building for about twenty years, he "suddenly" discovered that an essential part was missing – the middle part had to be completed so that it would connect the left and right towers. A year later it was all finished. The final stone had been placed in a structure that cannot be judged purely on architectural or functional grounds. The builder had declared it a "place of ripening." His work on it should not be confused with the busywork of an old man. From time to time he wrote from Bollingen to let his collaborator know how it stood with the things that were important in his life. In his letter to Aniela Jaffé of 18 March 1957 we read: "I finished painting the ceiling in Bollingen and worked some more on my inscription and – last but not least – I rewalled my well and cooked some good meals and found an excellent wine and bought it. That all relaxed me and cured me of a number of complaints."[105] This was medicine that the psychotherapist himself had prescribed, clearly a very effective prescription.

But now the years, the months, the days were numbered. The signs of approaching death began to appear – synchronistic events, "pure coincidences," one might say. When he no longer had the strength for his daily walk, he had himself taken for a drive. It was a matter of driving along little-used roads, taking leave of the landscapes of his home country. On one such occasion, on 6 May 1961, something strange happened. Three wedding processions of the kind that are common in the country were encountered. The car had to stop. The connoisseur of myths took this threefold "coincidence" for what it was, an announcement of his wedding with death.

Jung himself recalled the joyous element: the female dancers on Greek sarcophagi, and the death-wedding of the great kabbalist Rabbi Simon bar Yochai, of which the *Zohar* tells us. For Jung also, death was a marriage, a mystery of union *(mysterium coniunctionis)*. "The soul attains, so to speak, its missing half, it achieves wholeness."[106]

After weeks of illness, after a stroke, after weeks of weakness and lying in bed, Jung was granted short periods of refreshed energy, which permitted him individually to receive intimate friends, among them the Chilean Miguel Serrano, who painstakingly recorded his meeting with Jung (as also that with Hermann Hesse). To him, the old man whose dreams and visions were filled with boundary experiences confided:

"Today no one any longer heeds what lies behind the words ... the ideas that they are based on. And yet the idea is all that is really there. My work was after all mainly to give these ideas and realities new names. For example, take the word "unconscious." I have just finished reading a book by a Chinese Zen Buddhist. I had the feeling that we were speaking about one and the same thing and were just using different words for it. Using the word "unconscious" is not the key thing. What really counts is the idea that lies behind the word."[107]

The old man was sitting in a chair by the window. He was wearing a Japanese ceremonial robe. His thoughts, however, ultimately revolved around the Christian *mysterium*. The visitor found a book – Teilhard de Chardin's, *Le phénomène humain* – lying on a little table near Jung. This great nature philosopher and mystic, a French Jesuit unappreciated during his lifetime, was only really discovered in the sixties – and only for a short time, as it turned out.

Emma Jung-Rauschenbach (1882 – 1955) a year before her death.
"The loss of my wife has taken a lot out of me, and at my age it isn't easy to recover." (Letter of December 14, 1955).

On his eighty-fifth birthday, in the midst of the flourishing Jung family.

Asked if he had already read this work, Jung answered, "Yes, and it's a great book!" There is no question – the old man who had been written off by all-too-righteous critics as an outsider, as a gnostic heretic, himself knew well enough how he should be classified and toward what goal his labor had been aimed: "Above all, I tried to make clear to the Christian what the Savior is in reality and what the Resurrection means. No one in our day seems to know this any more or to remember it; but the idea continues to survive in dreams."

Not only in dreams – for Jung at least, in consciousness as well as in the depths of the unconscious. This was and remained essential for him, as inconsistent or indefinite as his statements as a doctor and a scientist have sometimes been understood to be. The inscriptions on his gravestone

in the Küsnacht cemetery bear witness to this. The top and bottom borders repeat the motto he had chosen for his house.

Vocatus atque non vocatus deus aderit

Invoked or not invoked, the god is present.

The right and left sides contain words from the great resurrection chapter of *First Corinthians* (15:47):

Primus homo de terra terrenus

Secundus homo de caelo caelestis

The first man comes from the earth and is of the earth;

The second comes from heaven and is of heaven.

Carl Gustav Jung died in the afternoon of 6 June 1961.

JUNG'S INFLUENCE ON THE INTELLECTUAL LIFE OF TODAY

Carl Gustav Jung's analytical psychology is first of all a way of knowledge and a method of psychotherapy through which psychologically disturbed persons can be helped. But it is not only followers of the Jungian school in the narrow sense who practice it, rather, it has a general cultural influence. In elucidating this influence, however, a host of difficulties is encountered. In her book on the

With his secretary Aniela Jaffé, co-author of his memoirs, in 1948 at the Casa Eranos in Ascona.

Below: Letter to his friend Gustav Steiner: "... when you get old, you are drawn into the memories of your youth."

Lieber Freund!
Du hast mit Deiner Annahme, dass ich schon genügend beschäftigt sei, nicht da=nebengerathen. Ich ertrinke in den Fluten von Papier. Du hast ganz Recht: wenn man alt ist, wird man in Jugenderinnerungen zurückgeholt von Innen u. von Aussen. Schon vor 30 Jahren wurde ich einmal von meinen Schülern veranlasst, eine Darstellung davon zu geben, wie ich zu meiner Auffassung des Unbewussten gelangt sei. Ich habe dies damals in Form eines Seminars getan. In letzter Zeit wurde ich verschiedentlich angeregt, etwas wie eine Autobiographie von mir zu geben. So etwas konnte ich mir schon gar nicht vorstellen. Ich kenne zuviel Biographien und deren Selbsttäuschungen und Zwecklügen und weiss zuviel von der Unmöglichkeit einer Selbstbeschreibung als dass ich es

Jung myth in our time, Marie-Louise von Franz comments:

"It is an extraordinarily difficult task to present C. G. Jung's influence on the culture of our time. While most individuals acquire influence first and almost exclusively in their own specialized field, Jung's creative new conceptions concern humanity as a whole and have therefore found a resonance in the most various specialized fields outside psychology. ... His work reaches beyond the academic sphere into all other areas of life, for Jung was interested not only in the special ailments

Opposite, right: With Ruth Bailey, who cared for the elderly Jung after Emma's death in 1955.

"You didn't go far wrong in presuming that I am already busy enough . . ." Letter to Gustav Steiner, December 30, 1957.

of the psyche, but rather more in the mystery of the psyche per se, and this is quite simply behind *all* the activities of man. No house has ever yet been built, nor any artwork created, no scientific discovery has been made and no religious rite performed, without the human psyche."[108]

Such a comment from the pen of Jung's close collaborator of many years can be accurately understood only if we do not equate *psyche* with consciousness. This term always implies a dimension of depth, which always involves the force of the archetypes at work in their creative or possibly also destructive aspects. We are speaking of the *unconscious,* described in the words of Marie-Louise von Franz as that "modern, objective expression for an inner experience familiar to mankind from the beginning, for the experience that out of our own inner world strange and unknown things come upon us that can abruptly change things from within, that we have dreams and ideas about which we feel that we did not produce them, but rather that they arise, alien and all-powerful, within us."

No wonder that in earlier times such effects were ascribed to a divine aura, a god or demon, or a good or evil spirit. Here a power is indicated that manifests itself in man sometimes in its positive, sometimes in its negative, aspect.

If asked at this point to come up with a concise formula indicating Jung's significance, on the one hand, and on the other, showing the basis for the influence of the founder of analytical psychology, we might well refer to a short text from the year 1955. In the diploma presented to Jung when the Confederate Technical College of Zurich conferred an honorary doctorate on him, we read these words of appreciation, cited at the beginning of this study, which already contain an indication of Jung's current and future significance: "To the rediscoverer of the wholeness and polarity of the human psyche and its tendency toward unity; to the diagnostician of the critical symptoms of man in the age of science and technology; to the interpreter of the primal symbols and of the individuation process of mankind." That the credit for having laid the scientific groundwork for the modern discipline of depth psychology rests with Sigmund Freud was also indicated at the beginning of the book. At the same time, Jung's specific achievement of having opened up new and vaster vistas, not least in connection with religion and spirituality, is undisputed. It only remains to question whether Jung's particular contribution has received the level of recognition that might be considered its due in light of the above words of appreciation. The prospects from time to time appear rather sobering. In the 1975 festschrift on the occasion of Jung's one-hundredth birthday, Theodor Seifert, the head of the C. G. Jung Institute in Stuttgart, made reference to the considerable dearth of information that exists in many professional psychological circles. In his view, Jung's teaching is only partly known. In the academic world, it is "hardly" taught. In colleges and scientific institutes, Jungian psychology is remarkably feebly, if at all,

Archetypes of death and life:

Left: Ta-Urt, the ancient Egyptian hippopotamus god who, in the death ritual, devoured the souls of people who were found too light on the scales of death.

Right: Demeter-Ceres, the Greco-Roman earth mother and producer of all life, and thus the personification of growth and development.

represented. A glance at the literature of depth psychology not expressly oriented toward Jungianism reveals a similar situation. Thus the following remark of Seifert also strikes us as rather sobering: "Unfortunately, one can only assume that the related questions are familiar only to persons close to analytical psychology. Our colleagues in other schools of depth psychology know very little of Jungian methods, clinical psychologists or other members of the profession in general nothing at all."[109]

Such comments remind one of Jung's own remarks on this subject. Even in the correspondence of his last years he complained that his ideas seemed to run "into an impenetrable wall everywhere" and that people, fully ignorant of his work, contented themselves with false notions about it, indeed with distortions and preconceptions.

Interest in the approach, methods, and results of analytical psychology is growing from year to year. There are many indications to this effect; for example, in the United States *The Collected Works of C. G. Jung* is making more rapid progress than the original German edition. Jung's works have been translated into more than twenty languages, including editions of the collected works in both French and Italian. In a study of the growing influence of analytical psychology in the United States, American psychiatrist and analyst Harry A. Wilmer comes to the following conclusion:

"Among teachers with a psychoanalytic background, a growing interest in Jungian psychology can be detected. Unfortunately, Jung's thought seems rather to repulse extraverted and logic-absolutizing minds, that is, technologically and scientifically oriented Westerners, psychiatrists being no exception.... Doubtless an aura of mystification and religious ecstasy has diminished and distorted the image of Jung and his work."

But today, Wilmer feels, even in psychiatry, more and more openness is starting to appear. Once the dust has settled that has been stirred up by the debates of "psychotherapists," Jung will at last acquire the position that he deserves. And what is that?

It is to be found in the effect of his

This wooden figure was carved by Jung as a model for the 1.1-meter-high stone sculpture "Atmavictu" ("Breath of Life"), which found its place in his garden at Küsnacht.

work as a whole, rather than in any particular specialized field that Jung's work has stimulated or inspired. It is to be found in that central and all-encompassing knowledge that touches upon all areas of life and understanding – the knowledge of the Self and the world. In brief, analytical psychology is first and foremost a contribution toward a universal vision of reality that encompasses man and the world, mind, and matter.

Jung provided a part of the answer in an essay written in 1929, in which he more precisely defined his position in relation to that of Freud: "In my picture of the world, there is a great outside and a just-as-great inside, and between these two poles, for me, stands man, turning now toward one, now toward the other, in order, according to temperament and makeup, to deny or worship now one, now the other."

Jung's typology with its attitudinal types of extraversion and introversion arises out of this basic view, as does his idea of psychic energy, which is also based on opposites, but which cannot be reduced to a sexually motivated libido in the sense of Freud's psychoanalysis.

The Self that is described in terms of its relationship to the "great inside" and the "great outside," however, ranges beyond and transcends this polarity. Jung's encounter with Far Eastern spirituality, ancient Chinese divination *(I Ching),* and alchemy all pointed the psychologist toward the one reality, which Jung after a certain point designated by the alchemical term *unus mundus* ("one world"). This refers to a reality that at one moment he described in psychodynamic terms, at another, as an object of physical investigation. This *unus mundus* was especially important in Jung's later work and was an important theme in the fruitful exchange between him and Nobel prizewinning physicist Wolfgang Pauli.

In this connection, we must mention the phenomenon of "synchronicity," which cannot be explained by the generally familar concepts of causality. Synchronicity refers to the relative simultaneity of two events that seem to be connected with

each other in some enigmatic way but admit of no causal connection. For example, let us say that some inner perception occurs or that some emotion is triggered and a little later or even at the same time, some event takes place in the outer world. Of course the notion of "coincidence" does nothing to illuminate such cases. The inner perception could not be the cause of the outer incident, to say nothing of the impossibility of the converse.

A clue to Jung's understanding of synchronicity is his remark that the approach of microphysics to its unknown material is analogous to the way analytical psychology gropes its way forward among the unknown factors of the psyche. Each discipline in its own way reaches discoveries that can only be conveyed in terms of antinomies. In other words, the matter under discussion can be looked at from two viewpoints. It may be that in their researches physics and psychology are ultimately concerned with one and the same object. Could there be a unitary cosmic ground that at times manifests physically, at times psychically? The significance of Jung's depth psychology for the exact sciences lies in this direction. Carl Alfred Meier, Jung's successor as professor at the Confederate Technical College of Zurich goes so far in upholding this point of view, and at the same time holds Jung's achievement to be so important, that he sees the latter as a psychological analogy for the approximately simultaneous discovery of the quantum effect by Max Planck or that of light quanta by Einstein.

Let us remain briefly with the factor called by Jung the "great inside," for it is of the greatest importance for our time that the knowledge of the primal images of being and doing, which were indeed experienced in earlier cultural epochs but remained undeveloped in terms of thought, should now be rediscovered and raised under the description of "collective unconscious" into the consciousness of scientifically thinking men and women. Psychologist Friedrich Seifert has written:

"Neither philosophical deduction nor metaphysical vision, neither investigation of outer facts nor scientific induction, has been the sphere in which has been newly experienced and expressed this knowledge of the mysterious relationship between the specific and the general, between the personal and the suprapersonal. It has rather been the sphere of individual inner perception. ... It is clear to anyone who knows the new psychology of the unconscious, not just from literary and intellectual opinion but from living experience, that more genuine force is emanating from the rich (if also of course partly still unclarified) empiricism of present-day depth psychology and psychotherapy than from most presentations in the field of pure philosophy. ... The psychological researcher, in a much broader than the usual sense, has become for the present the spokesman for this fundamental insight – to wit, psychology, for which the "reality of the psyche" (Jung) has become manifest."[110]

As the "interpreter of the primal symbols of mankind," Jung created a kind of grammar and a hermeneutics, or method of understanding, that make it possible to decipher the language of the unconscious and provide guidance for people undergoing the process of individuation and self-development. This means providing therapy in the broader

Left: The Nobel Prize-winning physicist Wolfgang Pauli (1900 – 1958), who kept up a lively correspondence with Jung.

Right: Dr. Carl Alfred Meier, born in 1905 in Schaffhausen, was once, like Jung, an assistant physician at Burghölzli in Zurich. In 1949 he became Jung's successor at the Confederate Technical College in Zurich. Between 1948 and 1967 he was president of the C. G. Jung Institute in Zurich.

sense of the word. (The Greek term *therapeia* means primarily "service," which could extend to service in the cultural sense and include health care.) From this point of view Jung's contribution was especially an anthropological one, a contribution toward a more profound vision of man, ultimately, a service to humanity. This is the primary concern of depth psychology and psychotherapy. Beyond this, Jung's contribution can be more

Jung listening to an Eranos lecture (1938) by Paul Masson-Oursel of Paris on Indian theories of the savior principle. (Cf. Eranos-Jahrbuch, *Vol 4, 1936).*

precisely characterized in terms of two further aspects, dynamism and interrelation.

By *dynamism* we mean that analytical psychology does not restrict itself to mere description of particular psychological factors. It is true that Jung's "psychological types," part of the typology developed during his early period, are descriptive in nature. Jung's work as a whole, however, goes beyond the processes of description and interpretation. It also seeks more than to restore temporarily lost functionality to disturbed individuals. Analytical psychology can be spoken of as dynamic insofar as it does not merely interpret man anthropologically or confirm him in his existing state but rather changes him by awakening him to his potential. Change here refers to change in the sense of a ripening or maturation of the personality of the sort that enters a decisive stage around the middle of life or in its second half.

Long before the popular media discovered the "midlife crisis," Jung had developed in his work the necessary anthropological and psychological basis for suitable treatment of this life problem. In simple terms, while Freudian psychoanalysis places the emphasis on resolving juvenile and puberty-related conflicts, analytical psychology can be regarded as a psychology of middle life, of aging, of the second half of life. The relevance of this focus needs no special emphasis, particularly in a society that is more heavily burdened than ever before by the problems of old age – and not only in regard to financial support for the elderly. Aging and dying have too long been taboos. And it is precisely in relation to them that the great theme of analytic psychology – transformation – becomes important. This is a theme that came to the fore, significantly, in Jung's own midlife period and that literarily marked his separation from Freud, when it appeared in *Symbols of Transformations*. For, as Jung already wrote in "Wirklichkeit der Seele" (Reality of the Psyche), "What happens in the secret hour of middle life ... is the birth of death. ... Becoming and passing away is the same curve." All in all, enough reason to focus more strongly on life's turning point.

In his work of philosophical anthropology *Was ist der Mensch?* (What is man?),[111] the intellectual historian Hans-Joachim Schoeps expresses his feeling that contemporary anthropological conceptions do not have the very integral quality that is needed today. According to him, they are at best partial teachings that stand in unrelated juxtaposition to one another. Now what is the case with Jung in this respect? Branded as an outsider, as a fellow traveler of heretical gnostics, mystics, and esotericists, is he not also a likely target for such accusations? True, Jung's approach is conditioned by his philosophical premises and by his place in intellectual history. Fateful and existential factors conditioned his life and his work. Any assertion, however, that he offers us another partial teaching that stands in unrelated juxtaposition to other psychologies and comparable views may be denied – for the following reason.

Jung's work is from the outset directed toward interrelation. This is already expressed in the therapeutic practice. In analytical psychology, the proverbial "analyst's couch" is passé. The analyst and the analysand are instead partners of equal status, participants in a dialogue. Instead of "free association" produced by one person and registered (ostensibly) with detachment – at least silently – by the other, in Jungian therapy there is a fully mutual exchange of question and answer, of reporting, of generating new reference points (a process known as amplification). The decision over whether to accept or reject a particular aid to understanding (for example, a dream) is up to the patient!

Interrelating, entering into dialogue, responding to a questioner – all these also mean being ready to be changed oneself, re-examining one's own point of departure. Anyone who simply wants to adhere to the word of the master has not understood, in relation to Jung, either the dynamic aspect or the interrelational orientation of his work. Moreover, it is necessary to take seriously what Jung once wrote to a Dutchman with whom he was corresponding when he expressed the hope and the wish that no one would become a "Jungian." "After all, I do not advocate any doctrine, but rather describe facts and suggest certain interpretations that I consider worthy of discussion. . . ."

Hasn't the well-meaning discussion and dialogue partner not long since been laid low by overeager Jungians? However that may be, the actual therapeutic practice should be a more convincing index than the behavior of followers from which the master is no longer in a position to distance himself. In any case, it can be affirmed that Jung developed his psychology through being open to discussion and through a process of dialogue with representatives of other disciplines. And as far as his therapy practice was concerned, it happened at times, in particular cases where he considered it appropriate, that he sent patients to colleagues with different doctrinal orientations, even to Freud himself!

The actual interrelational character of analytic psychology manifests at the point when Jungian psychology enters into an intellectual exchange, is stimulated by it, and itself conveys helpful impulses. Here are a number of examples.

The name of sinologist Richard Wilhelm has already been mentioned in connection with the *I Ching* and also in connection with the ancient Chinese initiation text *The Secret of the Golden Flower*. Wilhelm's work was of such great value for Jung because it explained a great deal for him and also confirmed what moved him most deeply. Not only was Jung encouraged to deepen his study of al-

Above: 'Genio loci ignoto' – *Olga Froebe-Kapteyn had this stone dedicated "to the unknown local spirit."*

Left: An Eranos symbol in the garden of Casa Eranos in Ascona.

chemy, he also encountered in the "science of the *I Ching*" that principle of synchronicity whose parameters go beyond the boundaries of ordinary causal thinking. The psychologist was compelled to look around for such another explanatory principle because the principle of causality seemed to him inadequate to explain certain extraordinary manifestations of the unconscious psyche. And since modern physics, within its own special field of study, has encountered the same problem, the curious situation arises that the adept of the ancient Chinese art of divination and the contemporary physicist, supported by the analytical psychologist, can enter into a concrete dialogue.

From this we can understand why Jung's exchange of ideas took place to begin with far outside the academic framework. In other words, the much-discussed "change of paradigms" had already been "tried out" decades ago. As a site for this kind of discussion and exchange, the Casa Eranos presented itself – an idyllically situated country house on the shores of Lake Maggiore in Ascona. Olga Fröbe-Kapteyn hosted the annual Eranos conferences there starting in 1933. Jung was there from the beginning and without wanting it he became the *spiritus rector* of the circle of speakers and listeners. "An interplay, a play of relationships, that yields a dynamic whole, a fabric of intellectual relationships" – thus the founder characterized the Eranos circle.

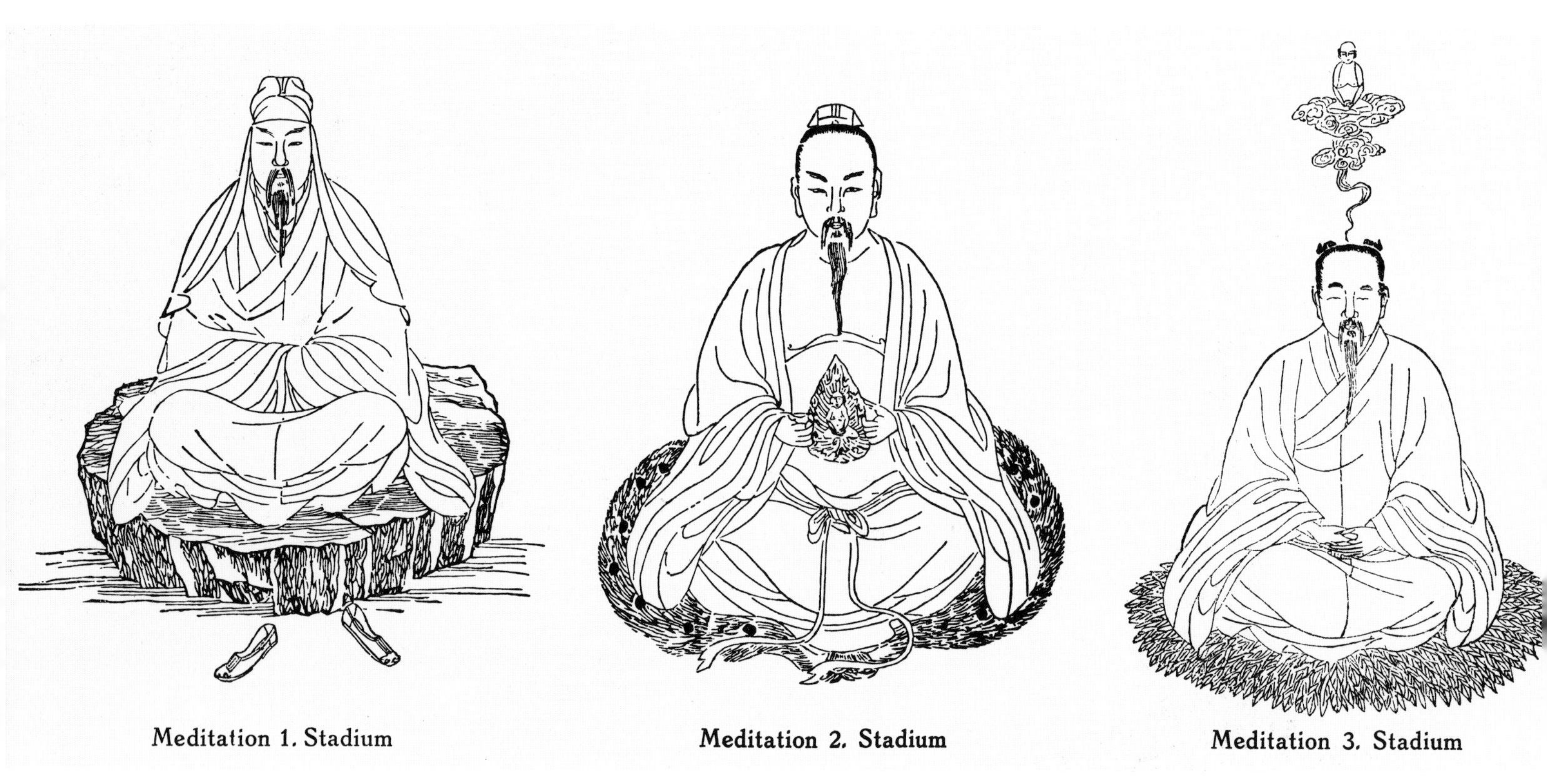

Meditation 1. Stadium

Meditation 2. Stadium

Meditation 3. Stadium

At the beginning, subjects from the humanities predominated; after the Second World War, the natural scientists – for example, the Basel biologist Adolf Portmann and the physicists Erwin Schrödinger and Max Knoll – increased their contribution. The first time the invitations went out for discussions at Eranos, characteristically, the theme was "yoga and meditation in East and West." Among the speakers were the Heidelberg indologist Heinrich Zimmer ("On the Significance of Indian Tantric Yoga") and the sinologist Erwin Rousselle, director of the China Institute of the University of Frankfurt. While two (former) Catholic theologians – Friedrich Heiler ("Contemplation in Christian Mysticism"), who later converted from Catholicism, and Ernesto Buonaiuti from the University of Rome ("Meditation and Contemplation in the Roman Catholic Church"), who was later excommunicated – represented the Western tradition, Jung's pupil and friend Gustav Richard Heyer lectured on "The Meaning and Importance of Eastern Religion for Western Psychology." Jung himself delivered "A Study in the Process of Individuation."[112]

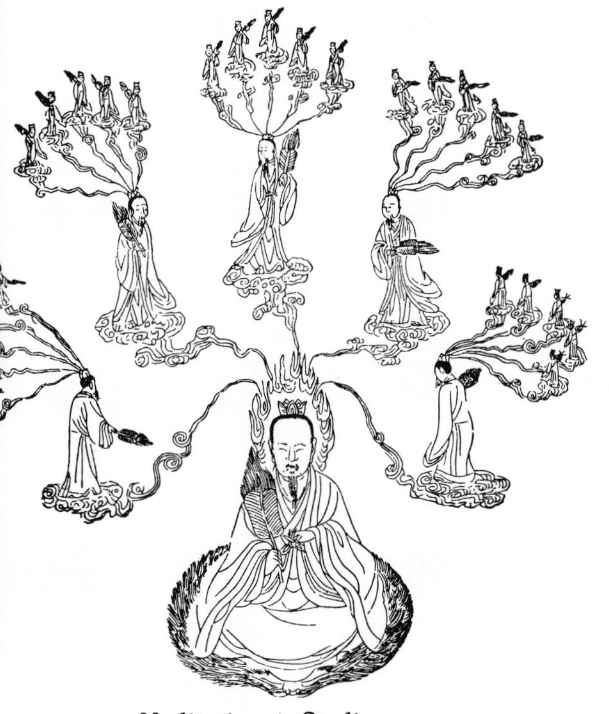

Meditation 4. Stadium

Between 1933 and 1951, when he presented "On Synchronicity" (enlarged in 1952 under the title "Synchronicity: An Acausal Connecting Principle"), Jung gave altogether fourteen talks in this setting. In the course of this activity, he many times showed his openness to the positions of others. One example of his encounters and intellectual cooperation with others is his years-long collaboration with Karl Kerényi, a Hellenist and an expert in ancient mythology and the ancient mysteries. Together the two published *Essays on a Science of Mythology.* The work of the two scholars elucidated the extent to which the mythology of the ancients is vitally related to what contemporary man experiences in the depths of his unconscious. It is not purely by chance that the curriculum for psychotherapeutic training in the Jungian school calls for knowledge of the imagery of mythology. In the prologue to the first volume of his collected works, Karl Kerényi writes:

"I chose for the title of this volume *Humanistische Seelenforschung* (Humanist psychic research) so as to characterize the particular qualities of a line of thought that, though for a long time I did not know it, would bring me together with Carl Gustav Jung. [Through my encounter with Jung] I became aware for the first time to what extent my mythological research is also "psychic research."[113]

Jung's collaboration with the ethnologist Paul Radin took a similar form. In cooperation with Jung and Kerényi, Radin published the Indian mythological cycle *Die Göttliche Schelm* (The divine trickster). Earlier, Radin had published a short work, *Gott und Mensch in der primitiven Welt* (God and man in the primitive world), in which he had set forth the ways in which analytical psychology had shown itself fruitful in his area of research. We should not forget that Sigmund Freud – for example, in *Totem and Taboo,* published in 1915 – had already laid essential groundwork for these studies. But whereas Freud saw his task as proving "a number of parallels in the psychological life of savages and neurotics," Jung directed his attention to the symbol-generating function of the unconscious. In this way, he succeeded in observing those archetypal powers that influence the human consciousness partly in a creative, partly in a destructive, manner – and not only the consciousness of neurotics. Marie-Louise von Franz, therefore, quite rightly points out that the discovery of the unconscious, that is, the collective unconscious with its power of generating

Dr. Ernesto Buonaiuti of Rome gave a lecture in Eranos in 1934 entitled "Symbols and Rites in the Religious Life of Some Orders."

Four stages of consciousness in Taoist meditation. (Cf. Richard Wilhelm's Secret of the Golden Flower*). From left to right: (1) gathering the light; (2) origin of a new being in the place of power; (3) separation of the spirit-body for independent existence; (4) the center in the midst of the conditions.*

This letter was written by Jung on March 1, 1952, to Dr. Daniel Brody, the director of the former Rhein Verlag in Zurich. Brody, once a journalist in Budapest, founded the publishing house in 1929. Since the beginning of the Eranos meetings in 1933, he published the Eranos yearbooks, which contain numerous works by Jung and his students.

Sehr geehrter Herr Doktor,

An dem Tage, an dem Sie das Jubilaeum des XXten Bandes Ihrer Eranos-Jahrbücher feiern, möchte ich in der Zahl der dankbaren Gratulanten nicht fehlen, sondern die günstige Gelegenheit benützen, Ihnen meine Gefühle der Anerkennung und Verbundenheit, die ich in all den zwanzig Jahren im Verborgenen hegte, öffentlich auszusprechen. Wer wie ich in der vorteilhaften Lage war, von Anfang an all die reiche Anregung, welche die gastliche Tafel des Eranos bot, geniessen zu dürfen, hat allen Grund, Ihnen zu besonderer Dankbarkeit verpflichtet zu sein. Waren Sie es doch, dessen grosszügigem Verständnis wir es zuzuschreiben haben, dass die vielen wertvollen Gaben und Geber, die zum Eranos in all diesen Jahren beigetragen haben, nicht wieder, wie sie gekommen waren, sich in alle Winde zerstreut haben, sondern in Bänden wohlgeordnet beisammen geblieben sind. Die zwanzig stattlichen Bände grüssen Sie von den Bücherschäften in vieler Herren Länder und künden - aere perennius - das Lob Ihres Idealismus und Ihrer Munificenz. Dieser Beitrag zum europäischen Geistesleben ist die kostbare Gabe, die Sie auf den Tisch des Eranos gelegt haben. Dafür sind Ihnen alle, die je von den Gaben des Eranos zehrten oder wenigstens naschten, auf immer zu tiefstem Dank verpflichtet.

Ich feiere im Gedenken diesen Tag mit Ihnen.

Ihr

stets ergebener

C. G. Jung.

archetypal images, brings about a doubling of our vision of the world and thus also an extension of our consciousness. And it is just this that constitutes the importance of Jung for our cultural and intellectual life. This at least hints at that aspect of Jung's thought that goes beyond medical psychotherapeutic treatment.

Many reached out toward Jung from within their own special fields. An example is the Swiss political economist Eugen Böhler. He drew the attention of business executives to the psychology of his compatriot and attempted in many publications to apply Jung's ideas to economic science. According to Böhler, economic life is not so much dominated by national goals as by collective impulses that have their origin in fantasy and myth. While production is the result of a rational process, consumption is dependent upon irrational impulses. Thus we have the unlikely case of a political economist, Professor Böhler, writing the introduction to a popular paperback anthology of Jung's writings on the archetypes of the collective unconscious and religio-psychological problems.

The results of Jung's researches in depth psychology have also been applied to the fields of political science and jurisprudence. As early as 1931 Dietrich Schindler produced a study of constitutional law and social structure that took Jung's ideas into account. And Max Imboden,[114] in his attempt at a psychological interpretation of national legal dogmas, has come to the conclusion that the three classical forms of the state – monarchy, aristocracy, and democracy – ultimately correspond to different stages of development of the collective unconscious. He makes the claim that democracy is a form of the state in which at least the majority should reach an adequate level of individuation, that is, self- realization. How wide a gap there may be between wish and reality in this case is of course another story.

Enough of examples, intended to give some impression of the breadth and depth of the present-day influence of Jungian psychology. We must not, however, omit to make some reference to the ongoing, intense mutual relationship between analytical psychology and theology. It is true that for a long time ecclesiastics approached the Swiss parson's son only with great caution, even though the dialogue had already begun during Jung's lifetime. In the three volumes of Jung's correspondence alone, the reader makes the acquaintance of about seventy theologians with whom Jung exchanged ideas – Protestants, many Catholics, and also Orthodox theologians.

The International Association of Physicians and Ministers came into existence in 1949. Today it is the International Society for Depth Psychology and has its seat in Stuttgart. At its yearly work conferences, where Jungians, along with other schools of depth psychology, are strongly represented, an attempt is made to attain an overview of different disciplines and in this way to counteract the widespread tendency toward self-sufficient specialized fields. In this context, theology and Jungian psychology enter into a fruitful dialogue, which is documented in the annual proceedings of the society.[115] This

With Olga Froebe-Kapteyn (1933), the founder of Eranos.

Below: At the legendary round table of Eranos with Erich Neumann (left) and Mircea Eliade (right).

At the round table with Zurich psychiatrist Hans Bänziger (1895 – 1956) and (at the right) the Protestant theologian Karl-Ludwig Schmidt (1891 – 1956).

Right: The French poet Paul Valéry visited Jung in 1933.

dialogue is not at all restricted to the practical work of caring for the spiritual welfare of church members, where naturally psychologists can make their expertise available. Also in questions of dogma and, particularly, bible interpretation, understanding of the archetypal language of images and symbols is seriously applied. How enlivening this kind of dialogue can be for theology has been visible in the work of the theologian and psychotherapist Eugen Drewermann.[116]

All in all, the comment made by Hans Schär in 1946 has proved to be true: "Anyone who concerns himself with religion today must know Jung's work and study it. It makes no sense to circumvent him; we can only go ahead in the direction he has set." In these words the theologian confirms what the cultural philosopher Jean Gebser had suggested before him when, in his book *Abendländische Wandlung* (Transformation of the West), he wrote:

"It appears to us that the future of complex [i.e., analytical psychology can reveal itself only when the general development of scientific thinking has reached the point where it can stand back from methods that are based too much on the demonstrable and too little on what is actually the case.[117]

Obviously, opinions will differ at this point. Anyone who does not wish to leave behind the domain of measurable, manipulable reality for the sake of broadening his horizon to the transrational level will be among those who relate to Carl Gustav Jung with skepticism if not disapproval.

Page 135: Jung and friends climbing the stairs in the garden of Casa Eranos (1936).

Voices and Testimonies

Carl Gustav Jung had one of those personalities that incites others to confrontation, even to side-taking, a personality concerning which opinions strongly diverge.

The following little chronology composed of voices and testimonies, conveys the diversity of his contemporaries' reactions.

Above: Hermann Hesse (1877 – 1962).

Right: Rainer Maria Rilke (1875 – 1926). "He in fact encountered the same realm of experience with which I have been occupied for decades."

Opposite: C. G. Jung with one of his doctor hats.

Sigmund Freud, 1907
I would like to repeat a number of things in writing that I have already acknowledged orally, above all that your person has filled me with trust in the future, that I now know that I am dispensable like everyone else, and that I wish for no one other or better than you to continue and complete my work.
Letter to Jung, 7 April 1907

Sigmund Freud, 1910
I hope you will loyally support Jung. I want him to acquire the authority that will entitle him to leadership of the whole movement.
Letter to Oskar Pfister, 2 May 1910

Sigmund Freud, 1913
I suggest to you that we completely give up our private relationship. By this I lose nothing, since for a long time I have been bound to you emotionally only by the thin thread of previously experienced disappointments. ... Spare me the supposed "duties of friendship."
Letter to Jung, 3 January 1913

Rudolf Steiner, 1917
A very meritorious investigator, Jung, who lives here in Zurich, has had recourse to some degree to transindividual, supraindividual, unconscious contents of the mind or psyche. ... A very meritorious realization, for thereby it is acknowledged that man in his subconscious is so constituted that he, in this subconscious, enters into relationship with a divine world.
Zurich lecture of 14 November 1917

Hermann Hesse, 1921
Jung, as an intellect as well as in terms of character, is a splendid, vital, ingenious person.
Letter to Hans Reinhart, May 1921

Oskar Pfister, 1922
I've had it up to here with the Jungian style. These so-called interpretations that parade all kinds of rubbish as higher psychic marmalade, all kinds of perversity as sacred oracles and mysteries, and sneak a little Apollo and Christ into every cockeyed psyche are completely worthless.
Letter to Sigmund Freud, 19 July 1922

Sigmund Freud, 1922
With your ever more thorough and ever more clearly demonstrated dismissal of Jung and Adler, you have for a long time given me great satisfaction.
Letter to Oskar Pfister, Christmas 1922

Rudolf Steiner, 1923
I will always recognize the conscientiousness and precision of a man like Jung. ... Only the development of today does not take these things completely seriously. But they must be taken completely seriously.
Lecture in Penmaenmawr, England, 31 August 1923

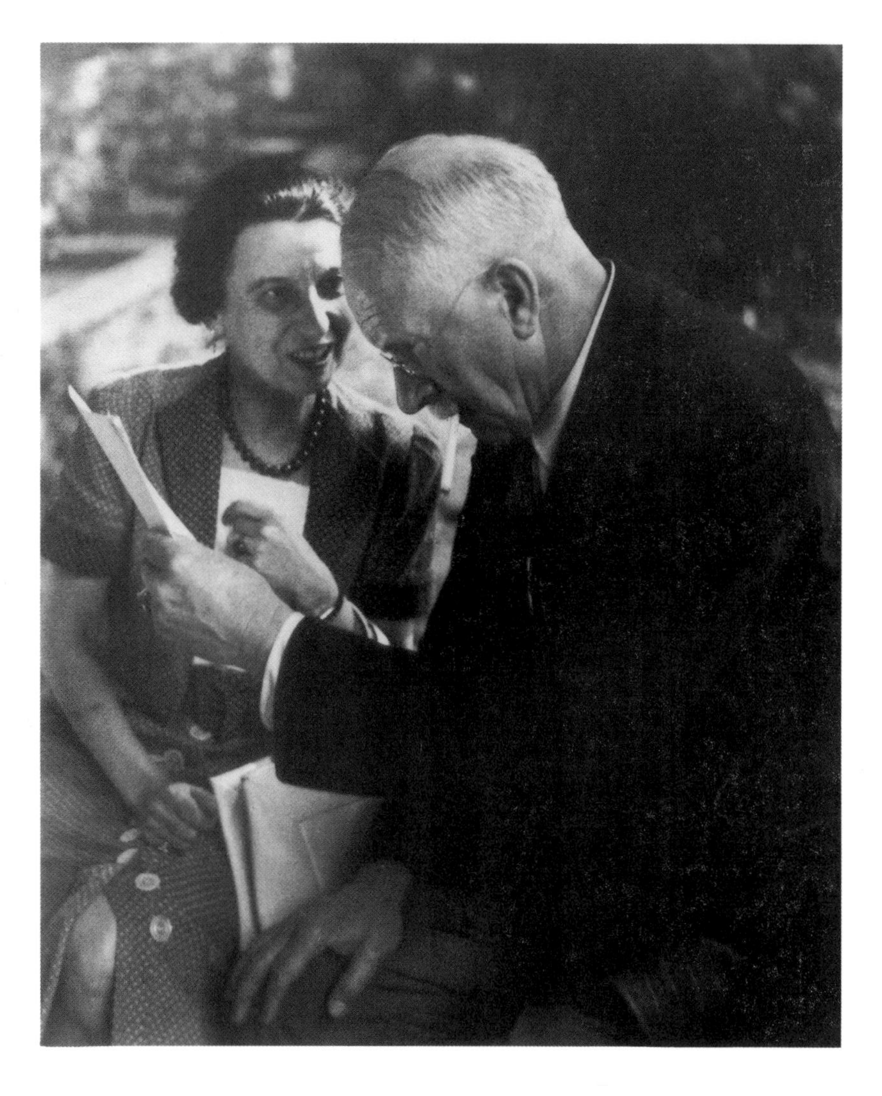

In conversation with Jolande Jacobi, known as the author of the book The Psychology of C. G. Jung *1939 (English translation 1973). Jung says about it in his preface: "She has succeeded in making a presentation that is free from matters of detail."*

H. G. Wells, 1928
As a writer who is concerned with all the questions of the human psyche and of the development of human society, I consider Jung's ideas, writings, and experimental results . . . a brilliant light in my darkness and a treasure trove for contemplation.
Neue Zürcher Zeitung, 18 November 1928

Richard Wilhelm, 1929
Between Jung and the wisdom of the Far East, there exists, not coincidental agreements, but rather a profound communality concerning the inmost view of life. So it is no coincidence that I, coming from China and completely filled with the most ancient Chinese wisdom, found in Dr. Jung a European with whom I could speak about these things as with someone to whom I was connected by a common ground. And it is with the greatest gratitude that I must acknowledge how many valuable ideas I owe to such conversations with the Zurich master. So in this way, I met Jung in China. ... since there was no direct outer means of transmission.

Dr. Jung is a Swiss far too sane and far too rooted in his native soil for him ever to go along with anything like a snobbish fashion for things Chinese.
Neue Zürcher Zeitung, 21 January 1929

Jolande Jacobi, 1940
Jungian psychotherapy is not an analytical procedure in the usual sense of the concept, though it keeps strictly to the prescribed medical, scientific, and empirical criteria of all related types of research. It is a *Heilsweg* in both senses of the word cure and salvation. It has all the prerequisites for being able to cure people of their psychic suffering and the psychogenic suffering connected with it. ... But in addition it knows the way and has the means to guide the individual man to his "salvation," to that knowledge and that fulfillment of one's own person that has always been the purpose and goal of all spiritual striving.
Die Psychologie von C. G. Jung, 1940

Heinrich Zimmer, 1943
The good fortune of finding Jung among the people who showed an interest in the things I [as an indologist] had to offer was the primary reason why I spent the next six years [after 1933] on the Continent, despite the ever-growing pressure and peril from the Nazi regime. ... Just the fact that nature made it possible for this unique and powerful exemplar of the human race to come into my life was and is one of the greatest blessings of my spiritual existence and altogether of my life on earth. ... I had met a human being the likes of whom I had never encountered before and the likes of whom I never would have thought to find in our times, but which was nevertheless long familiar to me from my conversations with sages, yogis, magicians, and gurus.
"Notes on My Life," *Merkur,* 1953

Olga Fröbe-Kapteyn, 1945
The collaboration of C. G. Jung with outstanding researchers in specialized fields and representatives of many disciplines that was made possible in the Eranos circle converted a variety of offerings into a coherent whole, a synthesis related to life and its deepest human problems.
Eranos Yearbook, vol. 12, 1945

V. E. Baron von Gebsattel, 1947
Without doubt Jung stands at the end of a movement that began with the schism in the Church in Germany. This movement, which like every historical movement can be understood only from its end point, carried a large part of Western humanity out of the protective space of the Catholic Church. ... Jung, in his retrospective view, is so aware of this loss that as a cultural psychologist he is regaining our freedom of understanding for the greatness, richness, and importance of the Catholic Church.
Christentum und Humanismus (Christianity and humanism), 1947.

Mircea Eliade, 1950
Jung is an enchanting old gentleman, not at all overblown, who is as glad to listen as to speak. What is the main thing I could note down here from our long conversation? Perhaps his bitter criticisms of official science. He is not taken seriously in university circles. "Scholars have no curiosity," he says, along with Anatole France. The professors are content to summarize what they learned in their youth and what does not create any discomfiture; what is important is that their intellectual world stays in balance. I sense, however, that fundamentally Jung suffers from this indifference. That is the reason he is so interested in scholars, from whatever discipline, who take him seriously, quote him, comment on his work.
Im Mittelpunkt (At the center) – Diary, 21 August 1950

Hans Trüb, 1951
Jung's creative accomplishment in the domain of scientific depth psychology can hardly be overestimated, nor, however, can his influence on practical psychotherapy be too carefully put to the test. For, also as a psychotherapist, he was above all a researcher.
Heilung aus der Begegnung (Healing through encounter), 1962

Martin Buber, 1952
In contrast to Heidegger and Sartre, Jung, the leading psychologist of our day, has made religion in its historical and bio-

Above: With the Indologist Heinrich Zimmer.

Below: At the round table of Eranos; right, Olga Froebe-Kapteyn (1939).

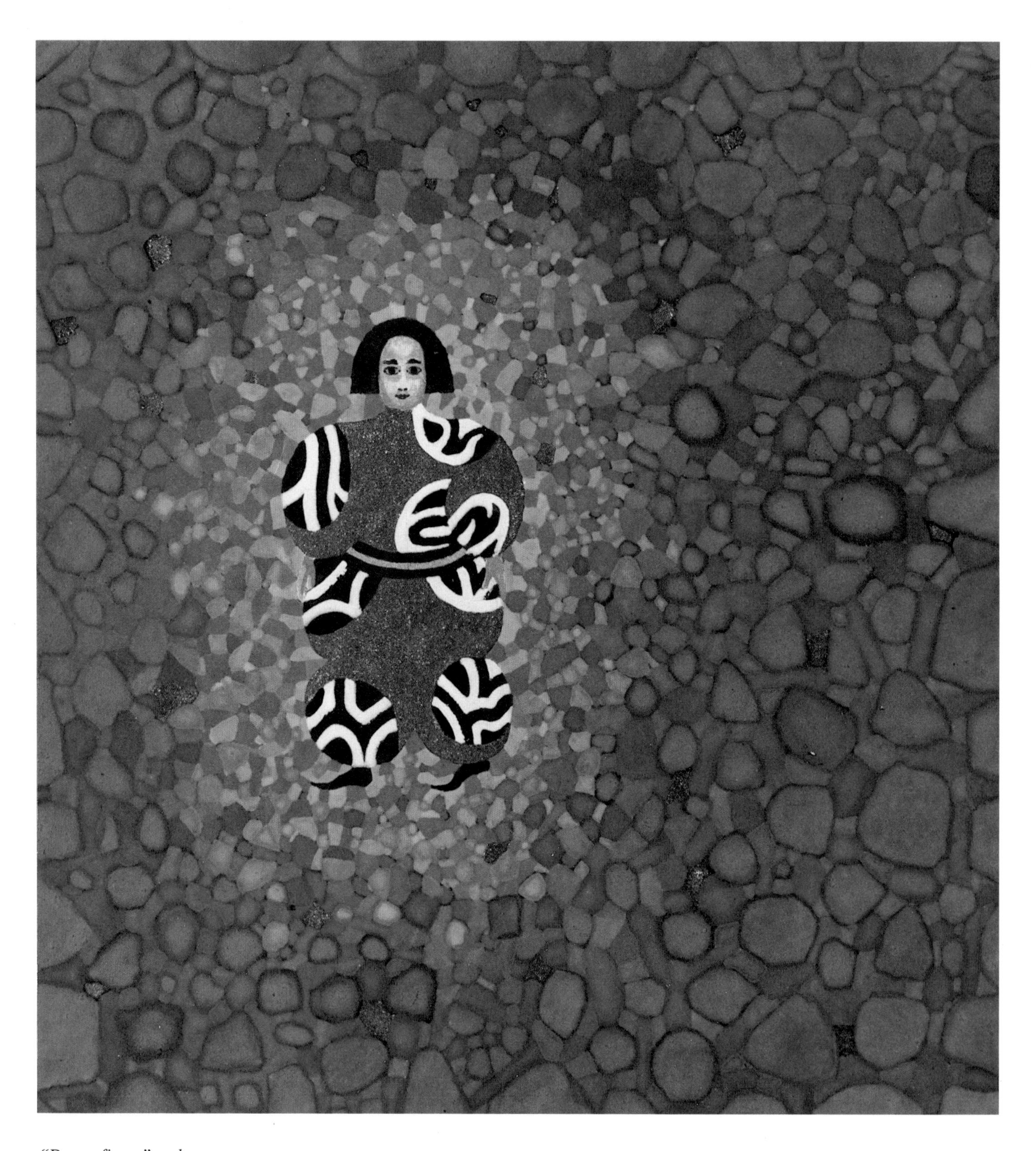

"Dream figure" as depicted by C. G. Jung.

"Knight with Sword," painting by C. G. Jung, dated 1917.

In conversation with Mircea Eliade on the occasion of an Eranos meeting (1950).

graphical structures an object for comprehensive consideration. ... What Jung can be criticized for is that in his treatment of religion he goes beyond the boundaries of psychology at the most essential points, but for the most part without noting, much less justifying, the fact that he is doing so.
Gottesfinsternis (Eclipse of God), 1952

Hans Blüher, 1952
The significance of C. G. Jung's discovery lies in the fact that he proved that there is something psychic-objective that exists at all.
Achse der Natur (Axis of nature), 1952

Hans Blüher, 1953
Freud is the actual and sole founder of scientific psychology. ... Naturally, one must also accord the description of genius to his apostate pupil C. G. Jung for his discovery of the collective unconscious.
Werke und Tage (Works and days), 1953

Rudolf Pannwitz, 1954
The entirety of Jung's work could, on the basis of its contents, be called a phenomenology, a comparative morphology and mythology of the functional psyche. He reaches into the broadest breadths and the deepest depths in order to come to know, comprehend, and guide the psyche through its critical obstructions and transformations through the whole of its imagic world. – *Beiträge zu einer europäischen Kultur* (Contributions toward a European culture)

Wolfgang Pauli, 1954
It seems to me extremely noteworthy that even the newest direction in the psychology of the unconscious, namely, that advocated by C. G. Jung, is a development in the direction of acknowledging the non-psychical in connection with the problem of psychophysical unity. ... Following his psychological intuition, he makes a connection with the concept of time by introducing in its stead the term "synchronicity." Here we are dealing with a first attempt to penetrate into a very new domain.
"Naturwissenschaftliche und erkenntnistheoretische Ideen vom Unbewussten" (Scientific and epistemological ideas of the unconscious), in *Dialectica* vol. 8, no. 4 (December 1954)

Ernst Bloch, 1955
There is nothing new in the Freudian unconscious. That became even clearer when C. G. Jung, the psychoanalytical fascist, reduced the libido and its unconscious contents entirely to primordiality.
Das Prinzip Hoffnung (The principle of hope), chapter 12.

Viktor von Weizsäcker, 1955
Jung has done extraordinary things for

psychotherapy by humanizing it and freeing it from its psychoanalytical arrogance. Through him it becomes clear what we are really dealing with in the cultural crisis.
Natur und Geist (Nature and mind), 1955

Erich Neumann, 1955
C. G. Jung is the only really great man I have met in my life, and as a teacher and friend over three decades he has provided me with ever new vital material for love and outrage, with the erratic quality of humanity-transcending nature itself. Encountering in a man, with all his weaknesses and in all his greatness, that which is greater than man and in which nonetheless everything human is rooted, was for me a decisive and direction-setting experience.
"Dank an Jung" (Expression of gratitude to Jung), in *Der Psychologe* (The psychologist) 7 (1955)

Jean Gebser, 1956
It appears to us that the future of complex [i.e., analytical] psychology can reveal itself only when the general development of scientific thinking has reached the point where it can stand back from methods that are based too much on the demonstrable and too little on what is actually the case. This observation will perhaps trigger some doubts, especially since it requires distancing oneself to a certain extent from the Cartesian way of thinking.
Abendländische Wandlung (Transformation of the West), 1956

Sir Herbert Read, 1960
A common misunderstanding sees in Jung a person who was originally a pupil of Freud's and later became disloyal to his master. Nothing could be more misleading. From the very outset there were differences in method and view that inevitably had to lead to divergent results.
Kunst und Kunstkritik (Art and art criticism), 1960

Paul Tillich, 1961
Many of Jung's ideas have been extraordinarily fruitful for theology and in particular for Protestantism. ... In that Jung explains the archetypes as originating also from biological, and thus also from physical, factors, he in fact enters upon the ontological dimension that characterizes the biological continuum. And this was also not to be circumvented if we consider the revealing power he attributes to the symbols in which the archetypes express themselves.
"Begegnungen" (Encounters) in *Gesammelte Werke* (Collected works) III, 1961

Jung with poet and literary critic Sir Herbert Read (1893 – 1968).

Overleaf, two pages: The tower at Bollingen today (November 1988).

Gustav Richard Heyer, 1961
Certainly his discoveries and formulations will be extended, modified, and, here and there, even corrected. But fundamentally

During a sailing party on Lake Zurich with Toni Wolff (1888 – 1953), who was his close confidante and collaborator up until her death.

what he achieved in his long life for medical psychiatry as well as for the development of a new image of man will remain.
Obituary in *Der Landarzt* (The country doctor), 1961

Otto Haendler, 1962
In memories of Carl Gustav Jung, there remains the strongest impression of his personality itself. It not only bore his gigantic opus but is also to a great extent the key to it. Jung was, to an unusual extent, original, vital, and immediate. ... He related to people, things, and ideas with his inmost personal being, and, just for that reason, in genuine meeting. This receptivity was connected with a direct impressionability and a deep capacity for suffering.
Wege zum Menschen (Ways toward man), 1962

Adolf Köberle, 1962
The theological inadequacy and the cosmetic errors that are associated with Jung's psychology should not ... lead the Christian church to close itself to his life work. For insights can be gained from Jung's psychology that are of the greatest significance for the renewal of the Christian church.
Christliches Denken (Christian thought), 1962

Erich Fromm, 1962
As far as Jung is concerned, one must admit that Jung understands far more about symbols and myths than Freud. It is in fact astounding how ungifted Freud was at understanding the forms of expression of the unconscious directly. ... Jung, however, is far more a relativist than Freud. For Jung, the problem of truth does not exist. Whether a religious belief is true or false is of no importance for him; psychologically it is always true. Such an affirmation, however, from the standpoint of logic, is nonsense.
"Die philosophische Basis der Freudschen Psychologie" (The philosophical basis of Freudian psychology), *Werke* (Works), vol. 8.

Walther von Loewenich, 1963
In Protestant theology, the development toward ever more pronounced abstraction is in full progress. But Jung will prove right: A religion without an image must wither away. ... A thorough exchange with depth psychology therefore seems to be one of the most important tasks of the theology of the future.
Luther und der Neuprotestantismus (Luther and the new Protestantism), 1963

Karl Epting, 1963
Jung and his work belong at once to the ecclesiastical and religious history, to the literary and art history, and to the zoology and anthropology of our times, but many years will have to pass before the new perspectives become generally visible in the individual sciences.
"Christ und Welt" (Christ and the world), Stuttgart, 8 February 1963

Maria Hippius, 1966
We may assume that Jung's anthropol-

Jung with Aniela Jaffé in the garden of the house in Küsnacht (1956).

Overleaf, two pages: The Jung family residence in Küsnacht, today.

ogy, which opens the gates of knowledge to transcendence on a scientific and empirical basis, will become more and more a self-evident factor in the education and renewal of the developed human being.
in *Transcendenz als Erfahrung, Festschrift für Graf Dürckheim* (Transcendence as experience, Festschrift for Count Dürckheim), 1966

Wilhelm Bitter, 1966
The accent in Jungian psychology is on the discovery of meaning through a primal religious experience. Here it joins personal psychotherapy, especially that of Count Dürckheim, as well as the logotherapy of Victor E. Frankl.
in *Transcendenz als Erfahrung* (Transcendence as experience), 1966

Miguel Serrano, 1966/68
The more I pondered the work of C. G. Jung, the more conscious I became that analytical psychology in a certain sense can be compared with a path of initiation. ... Jung's principal concern was bringing about a dialogue between man and the universe in which the personality, or ego, would not be destroyed.
Meine Begegnungen mit C. G. Jung und Hermann Hesse (My encounters with C. G. Jung and Hermann Hesse), 1968

Aniela Jaffé, 1968
Jung's humor and capacity for joy did not, however, preclude other moods, did not prevent resentment and grumbling from sometimes being the background music of daily life. Jung did not pass over any little slip, did not overlook even the slightest mistake; when he once began to think in terms of mistakes, there was no end to it. Fundamentally, this grumbling was a relief-producing rebuke of the thousand imps that meddled in his work and wanted to spoil his plans.
Aus Leben und Werkstatt von C. G. Jung (From the life and workshop of C. G. Jung), 1968

Opposite:
Even in old age, Jung never lost his cheerful spirit. This photograph is dated June 11, 1955, shortly before his eightieth birthday.

Ulrich Mann, 1970
We must try to do Jung justice by attempting to understand his often incautious and abbreviated way of talking from the point of view of his basic intention; that is, we should integrate his empirically achieved results into the required category of wholeness. In other words, we must take into serious consideration the fact that Jung did not want to produce metaphysical or theological arguments.
Theogonische Tage (Theogonic days), 1970

The Dutch student of Gnosticism Gilles Quispel (left) and the Swiss biologist Adolf Portmann at an Eranos meeting (1947).

Marie-Louise von Franz, 1972
Jung's work reaches beyond the academic sphere into all other areas of life, for Jung was interested not only in the special ailments of the psyche, but rather more in the mystery of the psyche per se, and this is quite simply behind all the activities of man. ... Thus it is no exaggeration to say that all the humanities and sciences, the religions, the arts, as well as the sociological and ordinary behavior of people appear before us in a totally new light as a result of the discovery of the unconscious.
C. G. Jung: Sein Mythos in unserer Zeit (C. G. Jung: his myth in our time), 1972

Victor E. Frankl, 1972
It cannot be emphasized enough what merit there is alone in the fact that he [Jung] in his day, and that means in the early years of the century, dared to define neurosis as "the suffering of the soul that has not yet found its meaning."
Der Mensch auf der Suche nach Sinn (Man's search for meaning), 1972

Alexander Mitscherlich, 1974
Jung's analytical psychology is in essence something like a doctrine of wisdom and not a science, which is definitely not meant as a criticism. On the contrary, it is one of the few alternatives to a positivism that has long since taken on in the world the character of a one-party system.
Frankfurter Allgemeine, 25 May 1974

Adolf Portmann, 1974
Getting to know Jung, experiencing the unremitting workings of his mind in daily conversation, experiencing the force with which he seized hold of new insights, being there when he drew to himself individual speakers who brought new themes into our circle [the Eranos conferences] and questioned them – these were impressions of lasting greatness.
An die Grenzen des Wissens (At the boundaries of knowledge), 1974

Carl Alfred Meier, 1975
Jung's achievement is so important that I do not hesitate to see it as the psychological analogy of the approximately simultaneous discovery of the quantum effect by Max Planck or of light quanta by Einstein.
C. G. Jung im Leben und Denken unserer Zeit (C. G. Jung in the life and thought of our times), 1975

Laurens van der Post, 1976
Jung was without doubt a great and inspired fellow being. He was a genius of intimacy. ... Jung's death has obviously not rendered him remote; it also has not, as strange as it may seem, reduced the physical presence of the man. Year after year he moves closer.
C. G. Jung, der Mensch und seine Geschichte (C. G. Jung: the man and his story), 1976

Page 152:
Bronze bust of Jung by Li Hutchinson, a student of Marino Marini (about 1955).

Detlef-Ingo Lauf, 1976
In the really quite short history of Western psychology as a science, Jung was the first to develop a comprehensive integral psychology, that is, a doctrine of restoration of psychic wholeness to the psychic and intellectual fulfillment of man. Its phenomenology of the inner structure of thought, of the psychological forms of knowing, of the empiricism of investigation, and of the conferral of meaning exhibits a striking resemblance to the philosophies and religions of the Asiatic world.
Symbole (Symbols), 1976

Alfons Rosenberg, 1983
Jung as an Aquarian type was able to jump from pole to pole in an authentic Aquarian manner and thus was able to interconnect psychological and religious knowledge in a jumpy fashion. Only someone with an intellectual pogo stick can follow his way of thinking or grasp his method.
Die Welt im Feuer (The world under fire), 1983

Franz Alt, 1983
In the search for meaning, C. G. Jung can be helpful. Like almost no other practical thinker of this century, he provides comprehensive advice for the most meaningful life – private and political, social and religious, holistic. ... I learned once again from Jung what I had lost sight of through a rationally overloaded theology: to understand afresh the psychic truths of the words and wonders of Jesus. This means religion as an opportunity for liberation and salvation, not as an instrument of intimidation or consolation. Religion as a possibility of discovering the soul and not as chance to repress everything connected with it. Religion as dynamite and not as opium. Through Jung it became clear to me that the essential question in relation to Jesus is not, What do I have to believe? but rather, What must I do and how must I live?
Foreword to *Das C. G. Jung Lesebuch* (The C. G. Jung reader), 1983.

"It happened more
than once that a passer-by stopped
at Mrs. Fröbe's
to inquire about the gentleman
who had just given out
with such a powerful and infectious
laugh – an infallible sign
of the presence of C. G. Jung."
(Gerhard Wehr: Jung – A Biography)

JUNG'S LIFE AND WORK		EVENTS IN SWITZERLAND AND ABROAD
Carl Gustav Jung is born in Kesswil, Canton Thurgau, Switzerland on 26 July, the son of Reformed Evangelical minister Johann Paul Achilles Jung and Emilie Jung-Preiswerk.	1875	Birth of Thomas Mann (June 6). Death of General Dufour (July 14).
Jung's parents move to Kleinhüningen near Basel.	1879	Bilateral alliance – secret agreement between Germany and Austro-Hungary.
Enters the Basel Gymnasium.	1886	Meeting of the three emperors (Germany, Austria, Russia) in Bad Gastein.
Studies the natural sciences and then medicine at the University of Basel. Passes the state examinations.	1895 – 1900	
Jung's father dies.	1896	
	1900	Freud's *The Interpretation of Dreams.*
Dissertation: "On the Psychology and Pathology of So-Called Occult Phenomena" (University of Zurich)	1902	
14 February: Marriage to Emma Rauschenbach in Schaffhausen. The marriage would produce five children: Agathe Niehus, Gret Baumann, Franz Jung-Merker, Marianne Niehus, Helene Hoerni.	1903	First flight by the Wright brothers.
Lecturer in the medical faculty of the University of Zurich (until 1913).	1905	The Moroccan crisis. First Russian revolution. End of Russo-Japanese War. Freud's "Three Treatises on the Sexual Theory," "The Joke and Its Relationship to the Unconscious."
Public advocacy of Sigmund Freud's psychoanalysis; beginning of correspondence with Freud.	1906	The Conference of Algeciras ends the Moroccan crisis.
Departure from the clinic. Beginning of private practice in his newly built house in Küsnacht. September: Guest lecturer with Sigmund Freud at Clark University in Worcester, Massachusetts. Receives an honorary degree there.	1909	The Bosnian crisis.
Wandlungen und Symbole der Libido (Transformations and Symbols of the Libido); after various revisions and title changes this would become *Symbols of Transformation.* Declares his split with Freud orally and in writing.	1910	Death of Edward VII; George V new king. Death of William James.
	1912	First Balkan War.
With his Zurich colleagues, Jung resigns from the International Psychoanalytical Association.	1914	Assassination of the Austrian successor to the throne Franz Ferdinand in Sarajevo. Beginning of the First World War, which on the Western Front soon became stalled in trench warfare.
Medical Corps doctor and commander of an English internment camp.	1916 – 18	Battle of Verdun (February to June). Battle of the Somme (July to November). Death of Austrian emperor Franz Joseph.
	1917	The United States enters the First World War. Russian Revolution (November 7).

JUNG'S LIFE AND WORK		EVENTS IN SWITZERLAND AND ABROAD
	1918	Peace of Brest-Litovsk between Russia and Germany. German offensive in France comes to a standstill (March – July). Retreat of the German army. Revolution in Berlin leads to the abdication of Kaiser Wilhelm II (November 9 – 10). Truce in Compiègne (November 11). General strike in Switzerland; the army steps in and ends strike actions (November). Influenza epidemic in Switzerland claims thousands of victims.
Journey to North Africa.	1920	Kapp Putsch in Germany (March 15 – 17). Beginning of the Greco-Turkish War. Founding of the League of Nations in Geneva.
Psychological Types	1921	
Death of his mother.	1923	France and Belgium seize the Ruhr Valley. High point of the inflation in Germany. Unsuccessful coup of Hitler and Ludendorff in Munich (November 8 – 9).
Journey to visit the Pueblo Indians in New Mexico.	1924	Death of Lenin (January 21).
Journey to visit the Elgonyis near Mount Elgon, East Africa.	1925	Hindenburg becomes president of Germany (April 26). Treaty of Locarno (October 15). German western border guaranteed.
"The Relations between the Ego and the Unconscious"; begins his study of alchemy.	1928	
	1929	Crash of the New York Stock Exchange (October 25) leading to a global economic crisis (until about 1932); worldwide unemployment.
Vice-president of the General Medical Society for Psychotherapy; president is Ernst Kretschmer.	1930	Death of Richard Wilhelm (March 1).
	1932	First International Disarmament Conference in Geneva. Violent unrest in Geneva causes sixteen deaths and many injuries. Geneva under martial law (November).
Following Kretschmer's resignation, takes over the presidency of the society.	1933	Hitler becomes German chancellor (January 30). The Reichstag is burned down (February 27). Law of empowerment (March 24). Germany's withdrawal from the League of Nations (October 19).
Foundation of the International Society for Medical Psychotherapy. Jung becomes president.	1934	Röhm Putsch. Hindenburg dies; Hitler becomes "*Führer* and chancellor."
Named titular professor at the Confederate Technical College of Zurich.	1935	Return of the Saar region to Germany (January 13). French-Soviet mutual-support pact (May 2).
Honorary doctorate from Harvard.	1936	Death of George V of England. Following the abdication of his successor Edward VIII, George VI becomes king (January 20). Hitler repudiates the Treaty of Locarno (March 7). German troops occupy the Rhineland. Axis Treaty between Germany and Italy (October 25). Beginning of the Spanish Civil War (until 1939).

JUNG'S LIFE AND WORK		EVENTS IN SWITZERLAND AND ABROAD
Terry Lectures at Yale University on "Psychology and Religion." Journey to India at the invitation of the British Indian government; honorary doctorates from the universities of Calcutta, Benares, and Allahabad.	1937	Death of Alfred Adler (May 28). Japanese invasion of China. Renewal of the Sino-Japanese War (until 1945). Cooperative agreement between Swiss unions and employers. Renunciation of the strike as a means of struggle.
Honorary doctorate from Oxford.	1938	Germany annexes Austria (March 13), Freud emigrates to London. Munich Conference (October 29). "Kristallnacht" in Germany (November 9). The atom is split for the first time, by Otto Hahn and Fritz Strassmann.
	1939	Swiss National Exposition in Zurich. Death of Eugen Bleuler (July 15). German-Soviet nonaggression pact (August 23). German invasion of Poland (September 1). Beginning of the Second World War (until 1945). Death of Sigmund Freud in London (September 23).
Psychology and Religion, book edition of Terry Lectures.	1940	German army takes Denmark, Norway, the Netherlands, Belgium, Luxemburg, and France (April to June). Air battle for England (August). Tripartite pact between Germany, Italy, and Japan (September 27).
	1941	"Operation Barbarossa": German attack on the Soviet Union (June 22).
"Paracelsica"; resignation as titular professor in Zurich.	1942	Battle for Stalingrad (July – February 1943).
15 October: Named full professor of psychology at the University of Basel.	1943	Surrender of the Sixth Army in Stalingrad (February 2). Battle of Kursk (July), the least major German offensive on the Eastern Front.
Withdrawal from teaching duties following a heart attack.	1944	Allied landing in France (June 6). Unsuccessful attempt to assassinate Hitler (July 20).
Honorary doctorate from the University of Geneva.	1945	Conference of Yalta (February 4 – 12). Founding of the United Nations in San Francisco (April 25). Hitler's suicide (April 30). Surrender of the German armed forces (May 7). Potsdam Conference (July 17 – August 2). The first atom bombs dropped on Hiroshima (August 6) and Nagasaki (August 9).
	1946	Italy becomes a republic (May 9). Paris Peace Conference (July 19 – October 15). Winston Churchill's visit to Zurich (September). New French constitution (Fourth Republic).
Establishment of the C. G. Jung Institute in Zurich; *Symbolik des Geistes* (Symbology of the mind).	1948	Founding of the state of Israel. Beginning of the Berlin blockade (August 4). International Declaration of Human Rights (November 4).
Gestaltungen des Unbewußten (The structure of the unconscious).	1950	Beginning of the Korean war (which lasts until 1953). European Convention on the Protection of Human Rights (November 4).
Aion	1951	Foundation of the European Coal and Steel Community.
Symbols of Transformation; "Answer to Job."	1952	George VI of England dies. Elizabeth II succeeds him on the English throne. Dwight D. Eisenhower becomes president of the United States. The first hydrogen bomb is detonated in the United States.

JUNG'S LIFE AND WORK		EVENTS IN SWITZERLAND AND ABROAD
Jung's *Collected Works* are published in New York as part of the Bollingen Series.	1953 ff.	Death of Stalin (March 5). Uprising in East Berlin (June 17).
Von den Wurzeln des Bewußtseins (On the roots of consciousness).	1954	Defeat of the French at Dien Bien Phu. Beginning of the Algerian war.
Honorary doctorate from the Confederate Technical College of Zurich. Death of Emma Jung (27 November).	1955	Foundation of the Warsaw Pact (May 14). Austrian state constitution (May 15). Death of Albert Einstein (April 18). Death of Thomas Mann (August 12).
Mysterium Coniunctionis.	1955/56	Suez crisis (October). Popular uprising in Hungary put down by Soviet troops (October).
Begins work on *Memories, Dreams, Reflections.*	1957	Establishment of the European Common Market (March 25). Launch of the first artificial earth satellite, *Sputnik I* (October 4).
"Flying Saucers: A Modern Myth." The German version of the *Collected Works* begins to appear in print.	1958	Proclamation of the Fifth Republic in France (October 4). Reform of the Swiss National Defense (December 22).
	1959	Charles de Gaulle becomes first president of the Fifth Republic (January 8). Social Democrats win seats in the German parliament for the first time (December).
On the occasion of his eighty-fifth birthday, Jung is named an honorary citizen of Küsnacht.	1960	Election of John F. Kennedy as U.S. president (November 7).
6 June: Jung dies in his house in Küsnacht. On 9 June he is buried in the Küsnacht cemetery.	1961	First manned space flight by the Soviets (April 12).

NOTES

Abbreviations for the works of C. G. Jung:

GW *Gesammelte Werke* (Collected works). Zurich, 1958 – 1970.

Br *Briefe* (Letters). Olten-Freiburg, 1972 – 1973.

M *Memories, Dreams, Reflections.* New York: Pantheon Books, 1963.

1. Marie-Louise von Franz, C. G. Jung. *Sein Mythos in unserer Zeit* (C. G. Jung: his myth in our time) (Frauenfeld, 1972), 16.
2. Jung as cited by Georg Gerster, "Eine Stunde mit . . ." (Frankfurt, 1956), 17.
3. *Symbole der Wandlung* (Symbols of Transformation), V, 13.
4. M 3.
5. M 10.
6. M 11 – 12.
7. M 4 – 5.
8. M 93.
9. M 28, 27.
10. M 42, 40.
11. M 108 – 9.
12. M 97.
13. M 99.
14. Stephanie Zumstein-Preiswerk, *C. G. Jungs Medium: Die Geschichte der Helly Preiswerk* (C. G. Jung's medium: the story of Helly Preiswerk) (Munich, 1975).
15. M 111.
16. Alphonse Maeder in H. F. Ellenberger, *Die Entdeckung des Unbewussten* (The discovery of the unconscious), vol 2, (Bern 1973), 893.
17. M 113 – 14.
18. Here one must think of Jung's affairs with Sabina Spielrein and Toni Wolff. See Gerhard Wehr, *Jung: A Biography* (Boston: Shambhala, 1988), 94 – 95, and A. Carotenuto (ed.), A Secret Symmetry: *Sabina Spielrein between Jung and Freud* (New York, 1982).
19. S. Freud and C. G. Jung, *Briefwechsel,* edited by William McGuire and Wolfgang Sauerlaender (Frankfurt, 1974).
20. GW III, 3 – 4. For more on the relationship between Jung and Freud, see M 146 – 69; see also Gerhard Wehr, *Jung,* 96 – 126.
21. GW III 3f.
22. See note 19.
23. M 149.
24. M 150 – 151.
25. M 155.
26. S. Freud and C. G. Jung, *Briefwechsel,* 612.
27. Ibid., 600.
28. S. Freud and Karl Abraham, *Briefe* (Frankfurt, 1965), 180.
29. Quoted in Aniela Jaffé, *C. G. Jung in Wort und Bild* (Olten-Freiburg, 1977), 63f.
30. GW V, 13.
31. M 175.
32. M 189.
33. M 181.
34. M 182.
35. M 188.
36. A. N. Ammann, *Aktive Imagination* (Olten-Freiburg, 1978).
37. Gerhard Wehr, *C. G. Jung und Rudolf Steiner: Konfrontation und Synopse* (Stuttgart 1972), now published as a Diogenes Taschenbuch, 52ff.
38. GW VII, 5.
39. Gerhard Wehr, *Heilige Hochzeit. Symbol und Erfahrung menschlicher Reifung* (Munich: Kösel, 1986).
40. Included in M 378 – 390.
41. *Studien über alchemistische Vorstellungen* (Alchemical Studies), GW XIII.
42. Foreword to the seventh edition (1937), GW VI
43. M 222.
44. M 238.
45. M 240, 244.
46. M 252 – 53.
47. Br III, 344.
48. GW X, 64.
49. M 225.
50. M 225.
51. Laurens van der Post, *C. G. Jung: Der Mensch und seine Geschichte* (Berlin, 1976), 80.
52. Br II, 298.
53. Gerhard Wehr, *Esoterisches Christentum: Aspekte, Impulse, Konsequenzen* (Stuttgart: Klett, 1975); *Auf den Spuren urchristlicher Ketzer: Christliche Gnosis und heutiges Bewusstsein* (Schaffhausen: Novalis, 1983).
54. Alexander von Bernus, *Alchymie und Heilkunst* (Nuremberg 1948), 95ff; See also Wehr, *Esoterisches Christentum,* 192ff.
55. M 205.
56. GW XII, 47.
57. GW XVI, 260.
58. See note 39.
59. GW XIII, 16ff.
60. GW XV, 63ff.
61. GW XV, 69.
62. GW XI, 571ff.
63. Erich Neumann, *Ursprungsgeschichte des Bewusstseins* (Zurich, 1949).
64. Gerhard Wehr, *C. G. Jung und Rudolf Steiner,* 133ff.
65. Jean Gebser, *Ursprung und Gegenwart,* in *Gesamtausgabe* (Schaffhausen, 1978), volumes 2 – 4.
66. "Yoga für den Westen" ("Yoga and the West"), in GW XI 575.
67. M 282 – 83.
68. On Jung's problematical relationship with Nazism, cf. Wehr, *Jung,* 304 – 30.
69. GW XVII, 201.
70. GW X, 178.
71. Br I, 180.
72. GW X, 613f.
73. Br I, 190.
74. GW X, 581.

75. GW X, 190f.
76. In this connection, see note 68; for a different emphasis, see Regine Lockot, *Erinnern und Durcharbeiten. Zur Geschichte der Psychoanalyse und Psychotherapie im Nationalsozialismus* (Frankfurt 1985).
77. Aniela Jaffé, *Aus Leben und Werkstatt C. G. Jungs* (Zurich, 1968), 92.
78. GW XL, 362.
79. BR I, 411.
80. Br I, 465.
81. Br I, 429.
82. GW XI, 4, 1.
83. GW XII, 23.
84. For more details, see Gerhard Wehr, *Die Deutsche Mystik: Mystische Erfahrung und theosophische Weltsicht* (Munich: O. W. Barth, 1988).
85. GW XII, 24.
86. GW IX, part 1, 78.
87. GW XI, 64.
88. See note 39.
89. Aniela Jaffé, *Der Mythus vom Sinn im Werk von C. G. Jung* (Zurich, 1967), 9f.
90. "Gegenwart und Zukunft" ("The Undiscovered Self [Present and Future]") (1957 and 1964), now in GW X.
91. M 331 – 32.
92. M 333.
93. Raymond Hostie in *Religionskritik von der Aufklärung bis zur Gegenwart,* K. H. Weger (ed.) (Freiburg, 1979), 177.
94. Br II, 114.
95. "Paracelsica" ("Paracelsus") (1942); now in GW XV.
96. GW XVI, 176.
97. GW XIV, part 1, GW XVII.
98. The individual contributions to these anthologies have been placed in a different order in the *Gesammelten Werken.* This is documented in the Bibliography in Volume XIX.
99. GW X, 339.
100. Preface to GW XVI.
101. Br II, 386.
102. Emma Jung and Marie-Louise von Franz, *Die Graalslegende in psychologischer Sicht* (Zurich, 1960).
103. Br II, 525.
104. Aniela Jaffé in M vii – viii.
105. Br III, 79f.
106. For more details, see Wehr, *Jung,* pp. 253, 341, 447, and Marie-Louise von Franz, *On Dreams and Death* (Boston: Shambhala, 1987).
107. Miguel Serrano, *Meine Begegnungen mit C. G. Jung und Hermann Hesse in visionärer Schau* (Zurich, 1968), 131.
108. Marie-Louise von Franz, *C. G. Jung. Sein Mythos in unserer Zeit,* 7.
109. GW IV, 389.
110. Friedrich Seifert, *Seele und Bewusstein: Betrachtungen zum Problem der psychischen Realität* (Munich, 1962), 282.
111. H. J. Schoeps, *Was ist der Mensch?* (Göttingen, 1960).
112. Now in expanded form in GW IX, part 1.
113. Karl Kerényi, *Humanistische Seelenforschung* (Munich, 1966), 12f.
114. Documentation and further information can be found in H. F. Ellenberger, *Die Entdeckung des Unbewussten,* 991ff.
115. The proceedings were originally edited by Wilhelm Bitter at the Ernst Klett Verlag, Stuttgart. They are at present in the charge of Peter Pflüger at the Walter-Verlag, Olten-Freiburg.
116. Eugen Drewermann, *Tiefenpsychologie und Exegese,* vols. 1 and 2 (Olten-Freiburg 1984).
117. Jean Gebser, *Abendländische Wandlung* (1943), now in the *Gesamtausgabe,* vol. 1 (Schaffhausen, 1975).

Bibliography

I. THE COLLECTED WORKS OF C. G. JUNG

1. Psychiatric Studies
2. Experimental Researches
3. The Psychogenesis of Mental Disease
4. Freud and Psychoanalysis
5. Symbols of Transformation
6. Psychological Types
7. Two Essays on Analytical Psychology
8. The Structure and Dynamics of the Psyche
9. Part I: The Archetypes and the Collective Unconscious
   Part II, Aion: Researches into the Phenomenology of the Self
10. Civilization in Transition
11. Psychology and Religion: West and East
12. Psychology and Alchemy
13. Alchemical Studies
14. Mysterium Coniunctionis: An Inquiry into the Separation and Synthesis of Psychic Opposites in Alchemy
15. The Spirit in Man, Art, and Literature
16. The Practice of Psychotherapy
17. The Development of Personality
18. Parts I and II: The Symbolic Life
19. Complete Bibliography of C. G. Jung's Writings
20. General Index to "The Collected Works"

II. SECONDARY SOURCES

Ellenberger, Henri F. The Discovery of the Unconscious: The History and Evolution of Dynamic Psychiatry. New York: Basic Books, 1981.

Frey-Rohn, Liliane. From Freud to Jung: A Comparative Study of the Psychology of the Unconscious. New York: C. G. Jung Foundation for Analytical Psychology, 1974.

Hall, James. A Jungian Dream Interpretation: A Handbook of Theory and Practice. Toronto: Inner City Books, 1983.

Hannah, Barbara. Jung: His Life and Work, A Biographical Memoir. New York: Perigee Books, 1976.

Hillman, James. The Myth of Analysis: Three Essays in Archetypal Psychology. New York: Harper & Row, 1972.

Hillman, James. Re-Visioning Psychology. New York: Harper & Row, 1975.

Hopcke, Robert H. A Guided Tour of the Collected Works of C. G. Jung. Boston: Shambhala Publications, 1989.

Jacobi, Jolande. The Psychology of C. G. Jung. New Haven: Yale University Press, 1973.

Jung, C. G., with Jaffé, Aniela. Memories, Dreams, Reflections. New York: Vintage Books, 1965.

McGuire, William, ed. The Freud/Jung Letters: The Correspondence between Sigmund Freud and C. G. Jung. Princeton: Princeton University Press, 1974.

Neumann, Erich. The Origins and History of Consciousness. Princeton: Princeton University Press, 1954.

Singer, June. Boundaries of the Soul. New York: Doubleday, 1972.

Stein, Murray, ed. Jungian Analysis. Boston & London: Shambhala, 1985.

Von Franz, Marie-Louise. C. G. Jung: His Myth in Our Time. New York: C. G. Jung Foundation, 1975.

Wehr, Gerhard. Jung: A Biography. Boston & Shaftesbury: Shambhala Publications, 1987.

Picture Credits

All art work done by C. G. Jung is protected by copyright laws and is published in this work by permission of the community of heirs of C. G. Jung, Küsnacht, Switzerland (© Erbengemeinschaft Jung).

Archiv für Kunst und Geschichte, Berlin: 4, 69 l., 96
Assistance publique, Hôpitaux de Paris: 23 top
Bau- und Umweltschutzdirektion Kt. Basel-Landschaft: 18 bottom
Baugeschichtliches Archiv der Stadt Zürich: 24 bottom l., 32, 105 bottom
Bernhard, Dora, Rom: 70 center r., 117 bottom, 121
Bernhard, Fritz (photo): 70 top l., 70 center r., 116, 117 bottom, 121
Bildarchiv Österreichische Nationalbibliothek, Wien: 29 l., 29 r., 39
Bildarchiv Preussischer Kulturbesitz, Berlin: 20 top, 21 top, 34, 86 r. (fourth from top), 90, 91, 92
Bouvier, Nicolas, Genève (photos): 52(2), 82, 83, 87(2), 98, 99
Brunner, Prof. Dr. Cornelia, Zürich: 40, 43, 48, 65 bottom, 66 top r., 70 bottom r., 72 l., 105 top, 110, 114, 115 r., 120 r., 126, 127 r., 143
Collection Jung-Institut, Küsnacht: 38
Dahlmann, Joseph: Indische Fahrten, Freiburg 1927: 84
EMB-Archiv, Luzern: 54
Erbengemeinschaft Jung, Küsnacht (©): 19, 28, 36, 38 top, 41, 42, 48, 50, 55, 58, 68, 70 bottom, 72 r., 79, 86, 123, 140, 141
ETH-Bibliothek, Jung-Archiv, Zürich: 19 r., 28, 36, 63 top, 70 center l., 86 l., 123 bottom, 127 l.
Familienarchiv Jung, Küsnacht: 2, 8, 12 r., 13, 16, 22 top l., 22 bottom r., 24 top l., 24 r., 38, 49, 59, 62(3), 64(3), 65 bottom, 66 top l., 66 bottom, 67 center l., 67 bottom, 69 r., 71 l., 71 center, 78 top, 88 center, 94, 106, 111, 112 top r., 113, 119 r., 120 l., 122 l., 138
Flury, Hannes D., Basel (photo): 15
Foto Münsted, Zürich: photo jacket cover
Franz, Marie-Louise von, Küsnacht: 78 l.
Gemeinde Keswil: 9
Gidal, Tim, Tel-Aviv (photo): 147
Glasenapp, Helmut von: Indien, München 1925: 85 top
The Goddard Library, Clark University, Worcester, Mass.: 35(2)
Historisches Museum der Stadt Wien, Wien: 30/31
Jaffé, Aniela, Zürich: 50, 71 r., 72 r., 116, 118, 123 top, 147
Jaffé, Aniela, Zürich [Ed.]: C. G. Jung: Bild und Wort, Olten 1975, 63 bottom
Jung, Andreas, Küsnacht (photo): 147/148
Karsh of Ottawa (photo): 110
Kenya Camera Studies, Nairobi, 1930: 66 center
Klinik am Zürichberg, Zürich: 6/7
Larousse-Giraudon, Paris: 23 bottom
Lauros-Giraudon, Paris: 26/27
Medizinhistorisches Institut der Universität Zürich: 12 l., 17 l.
Medizinhistorisches Museum der Universität Zürich: 33
Meier, Prof. Dr. C. A., Zürich: 5, 78 bottom r., 80 bottom, 93, 146
Migros-Genossenschaftsbund, Zürich: 102(2), 115 l., 125 l.
Mora, Jean-Claude, Basel: 73(4), 144/145
Musée du Vieux Pays d'Enhaut, Château-d'Œx: 45(3)
Museo Nazionale delle Terme, Rom: 125 r.
National Geographic Review, 1925: 67 top r., 1938: 85 bottom
Private collection: 14, 46, 47, 51(3), 88 bottom, 134 r., 140, 141
Ribi, Dr. med. Alfred, Erlenbach: 79
Ringier Dokumentationszentrum, Zürich: 44(2), 88 top, 108, 109, 117 top, 119 l., 151
Ritsema, Rudolf, Ascona: 152
Romeu, Stéphane, Ecublens (photo): 152
Rüedi, Ruth, Luzern (photo): 2, 6/7, 14, 25, 47, 51, 78, 80
Schweizerische Landesbibliothek, Bern: 89
Staatsarchiv Basel: 10/11, 20/21 bottom, (Collection Wackernagel 80), 123 bottom
Stiftung Eranos, Ascona: 86 r. (first and second from top), 95, 97, 100, 106 top, 107(2), 112 top r., 128, 129(2), 131, 132, 133(2), 134 l., 135, 139(2), 134l., 135, 139, 142, 150
Ullstein Bilderdienst, Berlin (Photo Ullstein – Sigmund Freud Copyrights Ltd.): 37, 86 r., (third from top)
Universitätsbibliothek Basel: 68(3)
Weltwoche-Archiv, Zürich: 122 r., 124, 137
Wilhelm Richard: Das Geheimnis der goldenen Blüte, München 1930: 130
Yale Picture Collection, New Haven: 101
Zentralbibliothek Luzern: 2563), 67 top r., 85 u., 136(2)
Zentralbibliothek Zürich: 17 r., 22 top r., 22 bottom l., 53(2), 56, 57, 60, 61, 74(2), 75(2), 76/77(6), 80 top, 81, 103, 104(2), 112 bottom
Zumstein-Preiswerk, Stefanie, Basel: 18 top, 19 l.

Acknowledgments

We wish to express special thanks to the following persons who helped us with information or provided generous support in the course of our pictorial research for this book: Dr. Heinz Balmer, Medizinhistorisches Institut der Universität Zürich: Dr. Dora Bernhard, Rom; Familie Bock, Uhwiesen; Prof. Dr. Cornelia Brunner, Zürich; Ursula Cadorin-Trüb, Zürich; Marie-Louise von Franz, Küsnacht; Dr. Beat Glaus, ETH-Bibliothek, Zürich; C. Gutzwiller, Staatsarchiv Basel; Aniela Jaffé, Zürich; Andreas Jung, Küsnacht; Dr. Lorenz Jung, Männedorf; Dr. Florian Langegger, Zürich; Pfarrer Helmut Mach, Laufen; Prof. Dr. C. A. Meier, Zürich; Dr. Christoph Mörgeli, Medizinhistorisches Institut der Universität Zürich; Jean-Claude Mora, Basel; Friedel Elisabeth Muser, Greifensee; Dr. P. Naeff, Basel; Dr. med. Alfred Ribi, Meilen; Dr. Michael Riedler, Zentralbibliothek Luzern; Rudolf Ritsema, Stiftung Eranos, Ascona; Stéphane Romeu, Ecublens; Agnes Rutz, Zentralbibliothek Zürich; Stefanie Zumstein-Preiswerk, Basel.